Dancing with the Queen, Marching with King

Dancing with the Queen, Marching with King

The Memoirs of
Alexander "Sam" Aldrich

Sam Aldrich

excelsior editions

State University of New York Press
Albany, New York

Cover photo of Sam Aldrich taken by Phyllis W. Aldrich in 2008.

Published by State University of New York Press, Albany

For information, contact State University of New York Press, Albany, NY
www.sunypress.edu

Excelsior Editions is an imprint of State University of New York Press

Production by Diane Ganeles
Marketing by Fran Keneston

Library of Congress Cataloging-in-Publication Data

Aldrich, Sam, 1928–
    Dancing with the queen, marching with King : the memoirs of Alexander
"Sam" Aldrich / Sam Aldrich.
        p. cm.
    ISBN 978-1-4384-3987-7 (hardcover : alk. paper)
    1. Aldrich, Sam, 1928– 2. New York (State)—Politics and
government—1951– 3. Lawyers—New York—Biography. I. Title.

    F125.3.A54A3 2011
    974.7'043092—dc22
    [B]   2011010858

10 9 8 7 6 5 4 3 2 1

Contents

Foreword

Alexander "Sam" Aldrich is a man born to great privilege who nevertheless chose a life of public service. Bestowed with the name "Sam" by chance when he entered St. Paul's School, Aldrich hung on to it for life, a small but firm affirmation that his path would be different from that of his forebearers. His grandfather, Nelson Aldrich, was America's "general manager" of the early twentieth century; as Senate majority leader, he had a big hand in creating both the Federal Reserve system, and—most un-Republican—the modern national income tax. His father, Winthrop Aldrich, was CEO of the Chase National Bank and ambassador to the Court of St James. And, most important for this memoir, his cousin was Nelson Aldrich Rockefeller, New York's forty-fifth governor and the dominant figure in state public life of his era.

Aldrich followed his father's path to Harvard College (after an interlude at MIT) and Harvard Law School. He began his career in a white-shoe firm, but then escaped the law to begin public service as an aide to New York City's police commissioner. In the NYPD he developed an interest in youth work and delinquency prevention, one area in which his cousin the governor later called upon him to provide leadership. Sam Aldrich also served Governor Rockefeller in various other capacities, first as an executive assistant and overall trouble shooter, and later as Parks Commissioner, a job in which he further developed his great passion for the environment.

The author remains loyal to Nelson Rockefeller even today, as he offers vignettes that enrich the governor's record, while debunking commonly accepted stories that diminish his luster. Aldrich's account of his leadership at the governor's request of the response to race riots in Rochester in 1964, and the failure to later apply the documented lessons of how to respond to similar emergencies, is particularly interesting in light of our post-9/11 preoccupation with disaster preparedness and response.

It is often forgotten that, for much of American history, civil rights was a Republican cause, not a Democratic one. Sam Aldrich's value to the governor as his representative at great movement events of the 1960s was enhanced because he was a member of the family. He clearly draws from diaries or other detailed contemporaneous notes as he reports here in great detail, more than half a century later and with great passion and pride, of his presence at the "I Have A Dream Speech" at the Mall in Washington, D.C., in 1963, and of marching with Martin Luther King in Montgomery in 1964.

Sam Aldrich was a man present as New York history was made, a player in state government, though not a transformative one. His life-long effort to achieve autonomy and self-definition was clearly not easy, and yet he is discreet in this telling, both about his public and his private life. His family, I am sure, will be happy to have this story, but other New Yorkers too are enriched because Aldrich decided to give us this account. As a result, we know a bit more about our state and the people that made it, and the promise it still holds.

Gerald Benjamin

Acknowledgments

These are the people who inspired, influenced, and otherwise assisted me in writing these memoirs.

Harriet Alexander Aldrich, born 1888, died 1972. My mother, who kept a diary every day of her life, devoted photographer, world traveler, who penned the renowned "Dear Girls and Alexander letters" to her children which form the collection stored at the Aldrich Library of the Rhode Island Historical Society in Providence, R.I.

Clem Williamson, my father-in-law, the best storyteller in my memory.

Judith White, writer, publicist, critic, chorister, who took my first draft and beat it into shape.

Ken Valentine, my computer consultant, who kept me from being driven insane.

Judy Drake, artist, chorister, who helped me select many of the photos in the book.

Field Horne, my neighbor in Saratoga Springs, who took the original material and prepared it for publication. Field also proofed my galleys and compiled the index.

The talented editorial staff at SUNY Press, including James Peltz, editor-in-chief; Amanda Lanne; Diane Ganeles; and my marketing guru, Fran Keneston;

My beloved sister, Lucy Aldrich Burr, of Mystic, Conn., the artist of my family;

Nelson Aldrich, my First Cousin once removed, who showed me years ago that Aldriches can write, and it was OK for me to try;

Steve Kennedy, the bold and brave Police Commissioner of New York City, who was the first man who trusted my judgment;

Nelson Aldrich Rockefeller who did so for 19 years.

Gwynneth Smith, Sharon Smith, Cynthia Fulton, and Sunny Wright, my wife's four wonderful sisters, whose support and understanding has always sustained me;

And, above everyone else, to my adored wife Phyllis Williamson Aldrich.

A. "Sam" A.

1

Dancing with the Queen

The two most exciting public events of my life occurred before I turned forty.

In the spring of 1953, when I was only twenty-five, I was invited to attend the opening of the new American Embassy residence in London. My father had been appointed ambassador by President Dwight D. Eisenhower two years before, and my wife Elizabeth and I had enjoyed the privilege of attending Queen Elizabeth's coronation and all the preliminary festivities. Even so, I was only somewhat prepared for what happened at this embassy event.

Queen Elizabeth and Prince Philip had been invited to the embassy party and had accepted, as had Sir Winston Churchill, who had recently been returned to service as prime minister for the second time.

The morning of the Big Day was devoted to preparing me for the ordeal of dancing with Her Majesty. My wife, my four sisters and their husbands were all there, and there seemed to be a general assumption that I would goof up somehow.

I was shown a small line on the floor of the ballroom where I was to be stationed as soon as my father danced once around the floor. When the moment arrived, I dutifully oozed into place and watched as my father and Her Majesty smoothly danced around and approached me.

Taken as the Queen arrived for the ball at the Embassy in Regent's Park, the night we danced together. She is being greeted by my father, the Ambassador. Photographer unknown.

"Ma'am," he said quietly to her, "may I present to you my son, Alexander?"

I do not remember her reply, but it must have been affirmative, and I placed my arm around her waist. I was frightened out of my wits, but immediately noticed how small she was, and how beautiful her complexion.

We danced a slow, two-step fox trot once around the floor, and by some miracle I managed to avoid breaking her or stepping on her foot, while making unremarkable small talk the whole time. She danced beautifully.

As we completed the mandatory single circuit of the floor, there was former Ambassador Henry Cabot Lodge standing on the place from which I had started. I had a sudden impulse to go right on by, but instead I stopped dancing, turned to the queen, and said "Ma'am, may I present to you Ambassador Lodge?"

She smiled prettily, thanked me for the dance, and was whirled away.

The entire event must have lasted for about ten minutes. Sadly, from the moment the dance ended, I could never remember anything either of us had said.

What I do remember was what happened next. I stood near the dance floor watching other people dancing for a while, and suddenly noticed I was standing next to a short, chubby man who was lighting an absolutely colossal cigar. He could only be Sir Winston Churchill.

I tossed aside my knowledge that British protocol frowns on speaking to someone to whom one has not been introduced, took a huge breath and said,

"SirWinstonIamtheAmbassador'ssonAlexanderandmy wifeandIlliverightaroundthecornerfromyourmother'shousein Brooklyn!"

He finished lighting the cigar, removed it from his lips, leaned over to me in a conspiratorial fashion and said. "I gave them a plaque!" Then he turned and walked away.

So, I had danced with the queen and chatted with Churchill. Would I ever again do anything more interesting?

The answer to the question above is an emphatic "yes!"

I also marched with Martin Luther King Jr., all the way from Selma to Montgomery, and that was even more interesting, lasted for more than a week, and was quite a lot harder to do.

2

Who is SAM?

I was born on March 14, 1928 in my parent's home at 15 East 78th Street in New York, which now houses classrooms of the Rudolf Steiner School.

I was named Alexander Aldrich.

I am Sam. Sam Aldrich.

And I love being Sam Aldrich.

In the fall of 1942 I was still Alexander Aldrich. I was fourteen, and my family sent me off to St. Paul's School in Concord, New Hampshire. On the first day of school, my first teacher, a rather large, self-confident man, came into class and said, "Boys, I want to know you all by your first names."

Since my last name began with A, my turn came first, but I was ashamed to say my name was Alexander, and my family nickname, Zander, was no better.

I tried my luck with the reply, "I'm very sorry sir. I have no first name."

"How sad," my teacher commiserated. "In that case, I'll call you Sam."

I came out of the class as Sam, and Sam Aldrich I have been ever since.

My mother was outraged, of course. Alexander was her maiden name. But I've always been happy that I'm Sam, because it's a wonderful, politically acceptable name.

1938 Long Island. Picture by my mother.

According to my mother, Alexander was a good Scottish name, and that was enough. I was given no middle initial, and I'm sure she felt I didn't need one: Alexander was sufficient. I was told about a time she attended a charitable dinner and found herself seated beside the current New York State comptroller, Arthur Levitt. He asked if she was related to Sam Aldrich. She pulled herself erect and replied, "Well, I've never really liked that name, but I am his mother."

But I've always been glad that I'm Sam. It's a name of the people, like Joe, and it has served me well.

Dancing with the queen of England was just a small function of the privileged life and family into which I was born. Expectations were that I would follow in my father's footsteps. He was Winthrop Aldrich, president and board chairman of the Chase National Bank, then the largest bank in the world. My mother was from California, and was one of the heiresses to the Crocker family fortune. She and my father had many social and professional obligations, and they traveled frequently and extensively, sometimes for months at a time.

I never really knew my father until we were both much, much older. When I was young I had first Wetherall, and then Shuff, our stately English butlers. They were the only male role models in my life for many years, and I was particularly close to Charles Shuff. He taught me what I needed to know as a young boy: how to shine my shoes and hold open a door, how to polish a table, polish silver, pack a bag; how to read the *Daily News,* and how to make a martini and a manhattan. He taught me manners, too, and basically all the necessary skills of a good butler.

He also taught me how to keep my mouth shut (which I immediately forgot).

I had a nurse who stayed with us until I was eighteen, but Shuff was the man I watched for cues as to how I should act. He was from England, and had served my grandmother from the time he was eleven, when he slept on a straw pallet beneath her pantry sink in London. His life's work was serving my family, but in my life, he *was* my family.

I was the only surviving Aldrich son. I had four older sisters, but I was the son, and the youngest child, too. That birth and gender order made a huge difference in my life. I was very sheltered, always being watched by nurses and maids and chauffeurs. My parents were frightened that I might die of an infection, or be kidnapped and held for ransom. Their first son, Winthrop, had died of acidosis in 1920.

I grew up in the early 1930s at the bottom of the depression, when people were selling apples on the street corners. The stock market crash of 1929 and the Great Depression that followed had less impact on us than on almost anyone else, a fact that dominated my entire childhood.

The Madison Avenue trolley went by my childhood home, which I considered modest: an eight-story brownstone. The first floor had a marble front and from there up it was brick, but it was in an area of brownstones, so that's how it was identified.

Our kitchen was in the basement, but the first four floors were for the family. We had an entrance hall, dining room and pantry on the first floor. The second floor in front was our family library, with a large living room in the rear.

Those rooms were above the dining room, so people being entertained would retire up the stairs from the dining room after meals. My parents' bedroom was in the back on the third floor, and in the front was the bedroom of my oldest sister, Mary. The fourth floor included my room, which was in the back; a smaller room for the nurse; and two large rooms in the front for my sisters Liberty, Harriet and Lucy.

My room was enormous; my sisters' rooms were tiny. There were bars on the two windows of my room, not to keep me in, but to keep Bruno Richard Hauptmann out. Those were the years after the Lindbergh toddler's abduction and murder, and my parents were scared to death that someone might kidnap me.

There were two more floors above our family space, where all the servants lived, and I was never allowed up there.

My nurse was Anna Williamson, and she stayed until I went away to college. She had a huge influence on my life: she was young and very Irish, and very adoring, affectionate, lively, and curious.

By the time I was six, my nurse, Anna Williamson, had become bold and confident enough about the safety of Central Park that she extended the range of my excursions all the way from the bench at the Seventy-Ninth Street entrance down to the lake north of the Seventy-Second Street entrance. It was possible, in the summer, to sail a small boat on that lake, and a child could clamber down a flight of steps to a cement pad that was right next to the water level. It was wonderful, and I was very comfortable with the whole arrangement, and equally careful about its potential risks (falling into the water, skinning my knee on the concrete, slipping on ice in the winter, etc., etc.) as frequently warned by Anna.

One glorious cold winter day in 1934, we trudged to the pond, and as I was accustomed, I went down to the concrete pad and stood transfixed, contemplating the heavy thick sheet of ice stretching before me. I was much too fearful to venture forth, and before I could turn back up the steps, a police officer across the pond blew his whistle!

Anna responded with olympic dexterity, ran down the steps and dragged me up to safety. I was stoutly maintaining that I had no intention of going out onto the ice, when the policeman came up to us.

To my utter astonishment and rage, he alleged that he had seen me *out on the ice!* Anna agreed with him!

My outraged denials fell on deaf ears. I was taken home in disgrace.

Years later, I was finally able to see the whole picture. The policeman's job was to protect dopey WASP kids from the attractive nuisance of ice on the pond, and from his vantage point across the way, the concrete pad probably resembled the ice; Anna's job was to protect me; Anna and the policeman were ethnic Irish; I was a frightened six-year-old. That I knew the truth was truly irrelevant.

Still, as the commander of the Juvenile Aid Bureau of the NYPD years later, I brought a special perspective to the job of distinguishing the guilty from the innocent.

My family employed three parlor maids, and we had a houseman named Berry—a little red-faced Irishman, who truly looked like a berry: short and stocky and red. He shoveled coal for us, and carried ice, and he lived on the top floor.

We had two other homes: one in Jericho on the "Gold Coast" of Long Island where we spent weekends and other holidays, and one in Islesboro, Maine, where we spent our entire summers. I was lonely for my family as a child, and sickly, but I had a great life, although it was expected that I would follow my father into banking, and events such as I recounted in the first chapter, "Dancing with the Queen," would be a regular part of my upper-class, well-traveled social life.

It was not expected that I would choose instead to follow my law degree with a master's degree in public administration, and then pursue a life of public service. I'm certain my father gave up on me while I worked to find an effective system to rehabilitate juvenile offenders in the mid-1960s, and went on to find an environmentally sound means for development in the Hudson River Valley.

There are many who will say that I owe whatever career path I've had to my family, and in particular to my first cousins, Nelson and Laurance Rockefeller, sons of my father's sister, Abby. Perhaps I do in some respects, but I studied and worked and had the drive and the passion regardless of Rockefellers—or other family members. My time in Albany as executive assistant to Nelson, and then a summer with him in Washington when he was vice president of the United States, was memorable, but no more so than other administrative jobs I've enjoyed.

Few would have predicted that at the age of eighty I would spend my time as a Stephen Minister, trying to listen, assist and pray with people in personal crisis, and singing in an Episcopal church choir, and that one of my recent delights was speaking to the Colorado elementary school classmates of my adored biracial grandchildren. I have parented nine children, in whole or in part with my first and second wives, and I grandparent eighteen. I love them all.

And who would have guessed that after the queen, the ambassador's son would insistently skip the dance cards and turn instead to a march with King?

3 .

I Have a Dream

During the summer of 1963, after the Birmingham church bombings killed a number of black children in Alabama, Governor Rockefeller realized that he needed to assert his leadership role in civil rights on both state and national levels, and he decided to make me his executive assistant in this area.

It never occurred to me to ask whether I had the qualifications to act in such a position. I had already demonstrated to him and to myself my ability to operate in interracial situations, especially in the New York City Police Department, where I had worked with the redoubtable Anna Hedgeman in the mayor's office, and in my state government role as the coordinator of the Harlem Office Building project. By then he also knew he could rely on my complete loyalty to him, as well as on my reluctance to do any grandstanding to promote my own career.

The very first assignment Nelson gave me in my new position was to deliver a proclamation to A. Philip Randolph, the head of the Civil Rights March on Washington on August 28, 1963, and to represent him personally at the march.

I flew to Washington on Tuesday·evening with George Fowler, the chair of the State Commission for Human Rights. He and I were commissioned to deliver a long proclamation to the marchers. I had drafted it, and Nelson improved it himself.

Everyone on the plane was a marcher. I sat between an NBC reporter and a bearded illustrator, who had designed all the posters or the march. In the limousine from the airport into Washington, I sat next to Mrs. James Farmer, the tiny, white schoolteacherish wife of the national director of the Congress of Racial Equality (CORE), who was a huge, angry dark black man. He was in jail in Plaquemine, Louisiana. She was remote and hard to talk to.

George and I checked into his room at the Statler, and I went down the elevator to buy a pair of sunglasses. When I got off at the lobby, there was the head of the whole march, the elderly, biblical A. Philip Randolph who had founded the Brotherhood of Sleeping Car Porters in 1925, three years before I was born. He was surrounded by reporters. Without a moment's hesitation, I charged up to him and I announced I was Sam Aldrich, representing Governor Rockefeller, and that I had a proclamation for him. He asked me to meet him in his room, 511W, in twenty minutes. The press asked if they could come, too, and he said yes, if there weren't too many.

I bought the sunglasses and took the elevator back to George's room. We paused there for a few minutes to check the 7 P.M. news and then started for the elevator again. Before getting there, George asked me if I had the proclamation. I had left it in his room.

We finally got straightened out and found room 511W. It was a tiny single room: I had expected a suite, with aides on telephones. Randolph was there with three reporters. I carefully unfolded the protective red cardboard case, and handed him the paper while he sat on the sofa. As a young man, he had trained for both the Shakespearean theater and as an opera singer. In his wonderfully deep voice and his broad A's, he read the entire thing aloud, deeply moved. I then expressed, as well as I could, Nelson's personal wishes for the success of the march and the mission it represented. We both thanked him for his courtesy to us, and then left to enjoy a Polynesian supper in Trader Vic's in the hotel basement.

George Fowler and I made a good team. He is a tall black man, a smooth, articulate graduate of the Cornell

School of Labor Relations, who had formerly served as deputy industrial commissioner for New York State, and was well known in the black community. As Nelson's first cousin, I represented the family's concerns. That evening we circulated systematically through the Statler lobby, being interviewed by radio people wielding tape recorders, embracing Anna Hedgeman from City Hall, greeting *Ebony* reporters, Democratic politicians, Brooklyn ministers and assorted March brass until well after ten.

I spent the night with my Harvard roommate Andre Rheault who worked for the CIA, and who drove me into the march the next morning. I paid a call on John Lindsay at 9 A.M. He was one of the very few congressmen who had the courage to hold office hours that day.

I left the Old House Office Building at 10 A.M. and walked about a mile to the Washington Monument. There I stood watching the buses arrive—a truly moving moment like watching the finale of the first act of Ringling Brothers Barnum and Bailey Circus, with the elephants pouring into Madison Square Garden, hooked trunk-to-tail. They were from all over: Detroit, Chicago, Allentown, Trenton, moving fast, people hanging out their windows, waving flags to say where they hailed from. The climax arrived when the Boston delegation arrived in a single line of thirty-three Greyhound buses, over three thousand people who had driven all night. The spectators gave them a big cheer. The parade marshals had expected five hundred buses, but to be safe, made provision for one thousand. Over fifteen hundred arrived.

After the Bostonians arrived, I shook off my fascination with the buses and crossed the street to the huge field to the north of the monument. As I did so, a loudspeaker on the official platform on the north end of the field announced that it was estimated that over ninety thousand people had already arrived and that traffic was backed up for thirty-three miles outside Washington, bringing in many more.

It took me about another twenty minutes to thread my way across the field towards the Lincoln Memorial. The people around me appeared to be mostly middle class, comfortably dressed in a conservative fashion. There were almost no small children, and very few under twelve. Roughly one out of five people was white, and a large percent of these seemed to be in their twenties. Some groups were hanging together in delegations, with armbands and leaders (for example, the Lower East Side NAACP). Others seemed to group as if from one large family, with breakfast in hampers. More than half the people were either sitting or lying down, and many were asleep in spite of a continuous chatter from the grandstand, which kept introducing folk singers (Joan Baez, Peter, Paul and Mary, Josh White, etc.) and celebrities such as the first black airlines stewardess, and occasionally announcing personal appeals such as that Mr. Washington Robinson could find his wife behind the reviewing stand.

The overwhelming impression was one of disciplined good humor, with a distinctly religious flavor. There was no hostility, no militant behavior, nothing but warmth, politeness, and a sense of shared satisfaction. Occasionally I would unavoidably collide with another person as I wended my way through the crowd. Every time, both of us would politely and genially urge the other to go first.

There was no possible way to reach the Lincoln Memorial except by using my now aching feet. I had agreed to meet George Fowler there at eleven, so I started down the north side of the reflecting pool. On the way, I stopped and chatted with many of the parade marshals and police, all of whom were from New York and members of the Guardian's Association of the NYPD. They were tremendously proud that they had brought all of their members, even the policewomen. One of them even remembered me as a deputy commissioner six years before. That gave me a real boot!

I arrived at the Memorial about 11:15, and was the first "honored guest" allowed under the rope at the foot of the steps. George arrived a few seconds later, and we sat in the two corner front seats, facing up the steps toward the main set of microphones at the speaker's dais.

There are two flights of steps up to the colonnade, separated by a flat landing about fifty feet wide half way up. Here were the mikes, in the center, with about five rows of seats on each side, for the absolutely ultimate chosen few. After we had sat for about fifteen minutes down in the front section for members of Congress and Supreme Court justices (none of whom showed up), Judge Hubert Delaney of New York suddenly appeared and, brushing aside the loud protests of ushers, marshals and other functionaries, escorted George and me up to Valhalla where everyone could see us. With the self-confidence of a pair of carnival barkers, George and I eased ourselves into the second row right behind Marlon Brando, Burt Lancaster, Harry Belafonte, Sidney Poitier, Sammy Davis, Jr., Ossie Davis, Peter, Paul and Mary, and Charlton Heston. Next to me, on my right, was a middle-aged lady representing all of the African American hairdressers in America. Next to her were two dignified rabbis from the American Jewish Congress, and a tall man with the four-star cap of a general in the Jewish War Veterans.

Then the march began. From where we were sitting, one couldn't see what was happening under the trees to the left and right of the reflecting pool. There was shade there, and in the heat it must have filled up first. There is a huge area, seventy-five yards wide, along the sides of the reflecting pool. For the next two hours, this space filled up, slowly but surely, and by 2 P.M. it was impossible to see grass, the whole way back. The crowd, in its good humor, collected by the thousands at the edge of the pool, doffed their shoes and socks, and gave their aching dogs a good soak.

Some of the speeches, from where we sat near the mikes, were hard to hear, unless the speaker was loud, clear and slow. In the gaps between them, we all chatted at length with the people around us. I reminded Charlton Heston of the time we met at the benefit première of *Ben Hur* when I was president of the Police Athletic League. He remembered, and then buried himself in a huge pad, spending the rest of the day sketching what was going on around him with a felt pen. He also chewed at his lower lip while sketching with such intensity I thought he would destroy it. Mary Travers occupied the seat in front of me for a while, wearing a tiny one-piece green woolen dress. She was over six feet tall with very long blonde hair, and having performed all day in the heat, she was perspiring so hard that the dress was sopping wet, leaving nothing to the imagination.

There were five moments during the afternoon I will remember forever. The first was when Roy Wilkins, head of the NAACP, invited the people under the trees to let us know they were there. Back came a roar that sounded as if it came from every state in the Union. That cheer had its own personality.

Next was when Walter Reuther, the white president of the United Auto Workers, started speaking. He hit exactly the note I felt so strongly, that discriminating against Blacks was just as big an insult to every white person as it was to him, and he said it with the fervor, timing, emphasis and vocabulary of a brilliant political peroration.

Mahalia Jackson was third, and was dressed in a bizarre costume that somehow evoked a drunken participant at a Princeton reunion—all orange and black. She sang near the end of the day, when the shadow of the Lincoln Memorial covered nearly half of the reflecting pool. Her first selection was a slow, religious piece with a quiet piano accompaniment. Then the crowd demanded a jazz number, and they got one with no accompaniment but the clapping of her own hands. Before she got through two measures, the huge crowd picked up the beat, and I could see everyone clapping this insistent, rock-solid jazz rhythm while she sailed like a clipper ship through the waves.

The great climax of the day came from Martin Luther King, Jr. It simply wasn't possible just to be an observer while he spoke. When he reached the part in which he repeated "I have a dream!" over and over again, and calling for his definition of real equality, every person there was on his or her aching feet, crying and cheering.

Impossible as it seemed at the time, it remained for the immense dignity of A. Philip Randolph to close the proceedings on the right note. In his quiet, deep, British West

Indian accent, has thanked all of us for coming, and told us
all to go to our homes in peace.

There was a temporary stairway off the back of the
memorial that allowed George and me to escape to the traffic
circle that led onto the bridge to Arlington, Virginia. It was
4:30, and I had a reservation on a 6:30 plane home. He returned
to the Statler, and I started limping across the bridge.

In Virginia, I collected a white minister from Hollis,
Queens, and we continued walking towards the airport, miles
away. Before fifteen minutes elapsed, an airport taxi appeared;
we hailed it, and picked up three more passengers, two from
the United Auto Workers and one from Nashville. All of us
were white, hungry, footsore, and inspired.

The Rheaults brought my bag to the airport, and we
had time to eat a big, welcome supper before I caught my
plane back home.

There had only been one other comparable event in my
life thus far, and that was the coronation of Queen Elizabeth.
One can only understand the march in that context, as an
occasion of the same magnitude. Most white people around
the country expected violence, which explained the dearth
of congressmen, but the crowd that came was positively
British in its self-restraint. The day was overpoweringly
American in every other way. It was a Baptist convention—
Jazz festival—country fair—Fourth of July celebration—Oscar
awards ceremony—visit to the Lincoln Memorial for 210,000
ordinary friendly people.

I feel truly sorry for everyone who wasn't there.

4

Marching with King

After the 1964 Federal Civil Rights Act focused attention on voting rights, there was an accelerated voter registration drive in the Deep South, aimed at registering substantial numbers of Blacks.

This drive met with massive resistance and delay, especially in the "Black Belt" of south central Alabama. The focus of this resistance gradually centered on Selma in late February, when first a black man, Jimmy Lee Jackson, and then a white minister, James Reeb, were murdered by people opposing the registration drive.

On March 7, 1965, "Bloody Sunday," six hundred Blacks marched across the Edmund Pettus Bridge on Route 80 south of Selma, bound for Montgomery, fifty-four miles away. Their stated purpose was to present a petition to Governor George Wallace, setting forth their grievances and demanding redress. As they reached the far side of the bridge, they were charged by a group of state highway patrolmen, beaten to the ground, and tear-gassed. Two days later a similar march, led by Martin Luther King, stopped short of the highway patrol and knelt in prayer. Then they went to court.

The following day the NAACP Legal Defense Fund sued in Federal District Court, seeking an injunction to prevent Governor Wallace from interfering with the next march. In a remarkable opinion, Judge Johnson of that court (a Southern

Author accompanies MLK and Coretta King entering Montgomery, Alabama on last day of Selma March, 1964. Picture by Moneta Sleet, now displayed on front wall of MLK museum in Atlanta, Ga.

Republican appointed by Eisenhower) found for the petitioners and spelled out the terms of the march: it would go from Brown Chapel in Selma to the State Capitol; any number could participate on four-lane highways, but the two-lane stretch of road (about half the distance) could only accommodate three hundred marchers.

It took about a week for the State of Alabama to exhaust its right to appeal. The second Selma march was finally scheduled to begin at noon on Sunday, March 21, and people around the country began to stand up and be counted.

I participated in the Selma March representing New York State Governor Nelson Rockefeller, my first cousin, for whom I served as executive assistant. Accompanying me on the march in an official capacity was George Fowler, chairman of the New York State Commission for Human Rights.

George Fowler and I called on Governor Rockefeller and recommended enthusiastically that he send both of us to the march as his representatives. There was some doubt in our minds whether we would be welcome to stay for the whole march, or just for the first day. But Nelson had no such doubt: if we went at all, he expected us to stay the whole way. He directed us to draft a telegram in reply to Dr. King, expressing his sympathy with and respect for the goals of the march, and setting forth his assignment of Fowler and me "to march in his behalf."

Friday was spent in a frenzy of planning. My most difficult decision was whether to bring Elizabeth, my wife, who was champing at the bit to come. After checking carefully, it appeared to be not only safe but appropriate to bring her, and I shall always be glad I did.

Saturday was a long hard grind. I realized that survival would depend partly on a really good pair of walking shoes, and my only pair was home in Chatham Center, Columbia County. I also wanted to bring as much other camping gear as I could scrape together, and above all I wanted to say good-bye to the children. On Saturday morning left New York City, driving up the Taconic State Parkway in a blinding, slippery snowstorm. I kept wondering if I would ever sleep again. We had an hour and a half at home to eat lunch, pack, and arrange for baby-sitters before beginning our history making adventure at 2 P.M.

Dan Button, the young and thoughtful executive editor of the Albany *Times Union* and *Knickerbocker News*, joined us at the house to travel with us. My state chauffeur, Paul Andress, drove, and I sat in front making last-minute calls on the car phone.

On the way to Newark, Dan interviewed me. As the ice piled up in patterns around the sides of the car, I told him my thoughts—that this march seemed to have a similar spirit to the 1963 March on Washington, but that its location in the Deep South gave it greatly added significance. I knew that our going on the march was to witness that problems existed all over the place and weren't limited to Alabama; that it was just as important for white people to be there as it was for Blacks; and finally that we were going to exhibit the concerns of New York State, its governor and ourselves.

While Dan filed his story from a phone booth in Newark Airport, we checked in and met our fellow passengers: George Fowler, Bob ("Slack") Johnson, a senior field representative from the State Commission for Human Rights and a graduate of Tuskegee Institute, Charlie Rangel, chairman of the Harlem Lawyers Association and a Democratic district leader. Quite a few people saw us off, including Percy Sutton, the black assemblyman from Rangel's district, who had cross-examined me for two days the previous summer in the case of the sit-in demonstration at the governor's New York City office. The flight to Atlanta was uneventful. Although I noticed nothing in the Atlanta Airport, Elizabeth got off the plane with Slack Johnson, a Black, and said she noticed some hostile looks. We all transferred to a crowded Convair which took us to Columbus, Georgia and in the process we picked up Jim Lawrence, a young neighbor of ours from Old Chatham who worked in the office of the New York State Budget Director.

In Columbus we were met by a station wagon from Tuskegee Institute. Jammed in like sardines, we rode for what seemed like one hundred miles but was actually more like forty-five, arriving at Tuskegee around 10:30 that night. We were met at the door by the institute's president, the quiet, careful-looking Luther H. Foster. Exhausted as we were, we realized that it was expected for us to go to his home, meet his wife, and discuss the general situation with them.

The Fosters told us of the debate raging on the Tuskegee campus between the moderates who believed in Dr. King's non-violent approach, and the militant Student Non-violent Coordinating Committee (SNCC). In spite of the latter's name, its leadership apparently believed in fighting back and in precipitating violence. The group's president, dour and bitter-looking John Lewis, had been leader of the black line on March 7.

Foster told us of a group of Tuskegee students who had gone to Selma the week before and had been "taken over" by a group of SNCC leaders. The students had resented the intrusion, and had learned to be much more wary and to stand up for their own opinions.

In spite of the interesting talk, we left as soon as we dared and fell into bed. I was wheezing with asthma and fatigue and general anxiety. I really wasn't sure I was physically up to the march, and the thought of having to drop out with bronchitis was discouraging.

We departed a little after eight the next morning. Selma is about one hundred miles west of Tuskegee on Route 80, and we bypassed Montgomery about halfway. From there on we traveled in comfort in our car for an hour, on the same road it would take some of us five days to cover on the way back.

About halfway to Selma we were followed for a while by an Alabama state highway patrolman. We didn't realize that the Tuskegee cars have a distinctive plate. I found out later in the week that the troopers had taken the plate numbers, and that the disapproval of the State of Alabama had been communicated back to Foster. I gathered that Tuskegee depends on the state for funding, and that the whole thing was pretty embarrassing to him.

The last seven or eight miles of the road into Selma was lined with military police from Fort Benning, Georgia. The best part of this sight was the frequency with which the pairs of policemen guarding the crossovers between the lanes of traffic turned out to be a white soldier and a black soldier.

We crossed the Edmund Pettus Bridge and found ourselves in Selma. We asked a group of soldiers where Brown Chapel could be found, and were ignored (probably orders). We finally found a friendly black man who directed us to the right place.

Brown Chapel is a rather small, shabby, crumbling brick church, on an unpaved, red clay back street in the poorest black section of town. A large pile of paper plates, cups and assorted garbage was smoking and burning right beside the back door to the sanctuary. A huge, aimless crowd of about four thousand people was milling around in the street. The press was everywhere, including several large TV trucks It was very difficult to see the front steps where the pre-march rally was to be held.

We went inside with some difficulty. The scene there was chaotic, and nobody seemed to know what was happening. A group of rabbis was sitting in folding undertaker's chairs beside the pulpit. Next to them, Constance Baker Motley, Manhattan borough president, was being interviewed on tape. Dan Potter, head of the Protestant Council of Greater New York, was there in his pearly gray vest, along with Paul Screvane, deputy mayor of New York City, Ralph Bunche, lots and lots of other brass, and hundreds of kids and plain folks, white and black.

Best of all, for me, was spotting Milton Luger, deputy director of the state Division for Youth. He had come down the night before and spent the night on the floor of an unheated house in the black section of Selma, with no water, and no mattress.

Gradually things took form, but it was a real struggle to get across to the march leaders who we were and that we represented the New York State governor. At one point Fowler tried to get out on the steps of the chapel while the speeches were in progress and was given a very hard time by the doorkeeper, Ben Owen from Birmingham, who would prove to very helpful to us later on the same day. Finally, around 1 P.M. we retired to the inside of the chapel and our names were read off by Andy Young, one of Dr. King's extraordinary young lieutenants, and we went out into the street to line up. Fowler and Rangel and I were in the VIP group; Elizabeth and Luger and Jim Lawrence and Slack Johnson and Dan Button were together about halfway back toward the end of the line. Eight abreast, we crept through the black section, down past the main business blocks, and then left onto Route 80 and over the bridge. Looking back from the top of the bridge, we were rewarded with the thrilling sight of five or six thousand people still pouring around the

corner, nearly half a mile back. It was a perfect day to walk:
cool and sunny, without a single bug, and with just enough
breeze. Len Chandler, a black folksinger in a yellow crash
helmet and a poncho made of a terrycloth towel colored blue
with white stars, began singing the songs that would sustain
us and keep us going for the next five days:

> Which side are you on, boy?
> Which side are you on?
>
> Old Wallace, never can jail us all!
> Old Wallace, segregation bound to fall!
>
> Pick 'em up and put 'em down
> All the way Montgom'ry Town.

He would walk backwards beside the lines, gradually falling
behind the pace of the march, singing each of the verses and
then the marchers would roar out the choruses. The only song
we all knew was the one which summed up the movement
long before President Johnson used it:

> We shall overcome
> We shall overcome
> We shall overcome some day.
> Ooooooh deep in my heart,
> I do believe
> We shall overcome some day!
>
> Black and white together
> Black and white together
> Black and white together now,
> Ooooooh deep in my heart
> I do believe
> We shall Overcome some day.[1]

---

[1] © Seeger, Caravan and Hamilton; words by Rev. Charles Albert Tindley,
1903; additional verses by Pete Seeger. Music: *O Sanctissima*, 1794.

Gradually the lines of marchers became less self-conscious, less disciplined and less like lines. About a mile or so out of Selma, I stepped out and dropped back to find Elizabeth. One of the marshals—not a federal marshal, but a young female volunteer with a SNCC button—threatened me with instant death, but I was adamant. I found Elizabeth in the line and walked with her for a while, and then the march stopped for its first rest break. We took this opportunity to amble back up to the front, or at least near it, where volunteers were dealing out peanut butter and jelly sandwiches and oranges and hideous glutinous rods of candy called energy bars. We managed to get a few of those and refreshed ourselves. Neither of us was too hungry, anyway.

When we started again, we made friends with Congressman Ken Hechler from West Virginia, originally from Long Island, who seemed to be a particularly good guy. After a while he offered to carry my pack, which George Fowler and I had been sharing, and we cheerfully allowed him to share our burden.

The afternoon was really quite uneventful, with absolutely no contact from the side of the road except the shouted taunts of a pathetic trio of teenage boys who gave the impression of simply being jealous. A man on a beautiful chestnut mare followed us with a movie camera for about a mile, finally dismounting and tying the horse to a large tin sign. When one of the ever-circling helicopters came close overhead, the horse bolted with the sign and caused an absolute uproar.

We had made arrangements (or so we thought) with our Tuskegee drivers to come back for us around 5 P.M., but as the hour drew near and it became obvious that we were still several miles from the encampment, we began to get quite anxious. At last, out of the blue, a taxi pulled up on the other side of the road and those in our group who were not marching the whole way jammed into it. They went back to Selma to find that Dr. Foster was unable to release his cars for the return journey, so they ended up taking the taxi all the way to Tuskegee. The following day Elizabeth and Dan

Button made it back New York together, although I didn't hear how they had made out until late Thursday.

As the shadows lengthened and the sun went down, we finally turned off the road to the right, walking over a hill past a small, rural African Methodist Episcopal Zion Church to a large field. We were about a mile south of the main road, on property belonging to a black farmer. The surrounding fields were used to grow cotton, and the land we were on was for pasture for his cattle. There were four large tents pitched quite close to each other: two colossal ones—circus size—a tan one for men and a green one for women. There were also two smaller tents, one with clear plastic sides that was set aside for the press, and one with canvas sides, which had no apparent purpose.

I spread out my slicker on the ground, collected all the gear belonging to Fowler and Rangel, and stretched out while they went out to "G-2 the situation." The next thing I knew, in walked Dr. King himself to say hello to me, and to send his thanks to Governor Rockefeller for sending us down. He was surrounded by a mob of disciples and press and rubberneckers, and seemed rather distracted.

Within half an hour it was pitch dark except for bare light bulbs fed by a portable generator that roared away near the small green tent. George Fowler finally found Rev. Ralph Abernathy, Dr. King's principal lieutenant, who sensibly gave the order that everyone should be fed, with or without a red armband. Until then, the badge of honor on the march was the armband, which signified that you had been elected to march the entire route, and entitled you to supper and bedding and other handy perks.

We got into line. The mess sergeants were a group of white ministers who had come to help from all over the country. Each of them wore a white card bearing his name and LOAVES AND FISHES in heavy ink. They were miracle-workers, too. Supper was spaghetti and meatballs, applesauce, green beans and coffee. They dished it out from brand-new garbage pails, and the food must have been cooked in Selma. It was brought to camp in a yellow Hertz panel rental truck and dispensed to us as we moved, surprisingly quickly, through a double line. These miracle workers never once ran out of food, and it was always on time.

After supper we struggled to acquire bedding. By some mysterious process, Ben Owen (who had given Fowler a hard time at Brown Chapel) took us under his wing, and by 9 P.M. we were the proud possessors of both air mattresses and Sears Roebuck sleeping bags.

After an abortive attempt to go to sleep in a corner of one of the big tents, we were all turned out while workers laid out long wide plastic sheets on the ground to insulate the sleepers from the dampness. As soon as we got back into the sack another man came by and announced that we were in the women's tent: we were told to move.

We were just about the last people into the men's tent, and it resembled Dante's Inferno. One bare bulb and two kerosene heaters were the only illumination. Several hundred men and teenaged boys were either trying to get to bed or were having a real good roughhouse.

George and Charlie and I watched the bedlam for about ten seconds before deciding that we would take our chances elsewhere. We tried the press tent, but it was completely full. Finally in desperation we settled in the mysterious fourth tent, which was completely empty. I unscrewed the only light bulb, we curled up, and the last thing I remember was the fleeting image of Ben Owen covering the three of us with extra blankets, which he had scared up by going all the way back into Selma. Since the temperature was well below freezing, we blessed him with chattering teeth and slept soundly the rest of the night.

Second Day: Monday, March 22

Our quite private tent was right next to the camp generator, and at 4:45 A.M. it suddenly turned on and woke me. Then the PA system announced, "We are on extra close security."

At that, I raised my head through a cloud of my own breath and looked out through the flap of the tent. A waning moon and the very first light of dawn lit the sky. A group of men, some with fixed bayonets and others with flashlights, were diligently searching a field about thirty yards away. In my befuddlement I decided that the worst thing I could do would be to get up, as they would no doubt shoot me on sight. The last thing I remember before going back to sleep was a strange, rapid snapping sound, like lots of people snapping their fingers. I found out several days later that a group of 82nd Airborne Division men, who were guarding us in a picket line around the field, had entered close to the tents to collect cottonwood for their fires. The camp security group had not trusted their movements and went to investigate. The snapping sound was the breaking of the cottonwood.

We woke at 5:20 for good. Everything was coated white with a hard frost. Several other refugees from the men's tent had joined us during the night. We soon learned that the horsing around had gone on most of the night in that tent, and that the leaders of the march were pretty sore about it. It didn't happen again. Ben Owen appeared right away, collected all our gear including the pack, and stowed it in a Hertz trailer. The sun was coming up and it looked like another really nice day was ahead. Aware of the danger of sunburn, I slathered my pale skin, especially my nose, with zinc oxide ointment, and put on my yellow slicker sou'wester from Dark Harbor, with the long end facing front to shade my face. In this costume I was discovered by Phil Sandlen, the tough young UPI photographer, while I was having breakfast with Ben and a lady friend of his, Lilie Brown. Breakfast, courtesy of Loaves and Fishes, was "thick and stick" oatmeal, canned milk, sugar, bread with oleo and jam, and coffee. Phil's photo of me got national distribution and was designated Picture of the Week in the *Amsterdam News*, the Harlem newspaper.

There was a long cold wait after breakfast. The sun came up in a clear sky, and at 7:30 we assembled into lines of four around the communications truck. There were still about six hundred people in all. While we were waiting to step off for the march, Andy Young came back and asked me to march in the second line, right behind Abernathy and Dr. King. I found myself walking next to a pretty girl, Ponchita Pierce, a staff member of Johnson Publications which published both *Ebony* and *Jet*, popular magazines for Blacks. The other two in our line were a young minister from Chicago and a bright Jewish New Yorker named Henry Schwarzschild. We stepped off at eight on the dot, Abernathy and Dr. King reading the Birmingham newspaper which reported on the finding of several dynamite bombs up there.

Within half an hour the line was joined by a second beautiful girl, one Sharon Mennen from Chicago, who was on the SCLC staff. Both Mennen and Pierce were interested in opera, and were intrigued by my having been to *Tosca* two nights before in New York. In spite of my zinc oxide appearance, I was able to enjoy the illusion that I was really the only James Bond in the whole line of march. Oh well; my fantasy was short-lived.

The only unusual event of the morning was being the target of a leaflet raid by the "Confederate Air Force." A plane buzzed us dropping sheets of yellow paper that demanded outside agitators go home. The press paid more attention to this than did the marchers.

It took us until about 11:30 to reach the point where the road narrowed to two lanes, and it was at that point that one of the most moving moments of the whole march occurred: the selection of the chosen three hundred. Andy Young took over, first asking those who were big enough to relinquish the privilege of continuing, to stand aside. A surprising number did so. Then one of the white women called out a suggestion that all the white people step out. Andy answered first that the march needed white people as protection. Then he realized that this was not the right answer, and in a moment of beautiful eloquence that I cannot recapture, he summed up the whole march as not just a black effort or an Alabama problem, but one affecting all people, white and black, north and south. He said we needed representatives from all over the country and from every race.

Somehow it was decided to choose 280 Alabama Blacks, mostly from Selma, and twenty national representatives. A list of the twenty was read off, and Fowler and Rangel and I were all on it, as were a union official, a nun, a one legged white man on crutches named Jim Leatherer, a blind man with his sister and seventy-two-year-old mother, a Peace Corps official, and a gaggle of ministers of assorted faiths. I think there were thirteen or fourteen white people who did the whole fifty-four-mile march.

While this selection process was being conducted, I was discovered by Paris TV. I was interviewed by the roadside (*en français, s'il vous plait*) on tape and film.

We stepped off again around noontime, this time three abreast. Leaders tried to keep the women in the middle with men on the outside. Charlie Rangel and I surrounded a snappy young black woman, Elaine Johnson, who lived in Newark, New Jersey, and had two children, but whose mother lived in Selma—and so was counted as an Alabaman. Fowler was right behind us. We crossed into two-lane territory, being carefully counted by the staff, by federal marshals and by Alabama authorities. There were exactly three hundred of us.

After a mile or so, we broke for lunch in a sandy gully, and Loaves and Fishes produced the usual rib-sticking meal of an apple, peanut butter sandwiches and energy bars. A water truck appeared, dispensing a clear liquid tasting of gasoline. For two days we drank the stuff until the 82nd Airborne Division condemned it as unfit for human consumption. We called it the oatmeal truck.

We set off again after lunch, and soon came to a small crossroads with a general store and an appallingly primitive "separate but equal" school: a single room, a tin roof, busted steps, and concrete pilings. One of the best excuses for the march might have been simply to publicize the existence of that one school.

We passed an infrequent shack, each with its pathetic cluster of Blacks on the porch. To each we yelled "Freedom!" and waved. Late that afternoon we passed a wretched, dried out field where a herd of scrawny cattle grazed. I shouted

"Freedom!" and waved at the cows. Anything for a laugh and a release of the tension we felt.

From lunch to dusk we stepped up the pace. Dr. King had left us to go to Cleveland for a fund-raising rally, and Bevel and Young were out front. I began to get to know our Alabama state highway patrolmen. There were three in particular. The first was a lean, quite handsome corporal, with a flair for waving cars past. He had the cruelest eyes I have ever seen, a shiny, snake's pair of eyes that I never hope to see in a squad room.

The second was a young guy with a particularly arrogant laugh and a long pale cigar that stuck straight out of his face.

The third was a mournfully sinister man with lips that turned down at the corners and whose whole face was constantly contorted with a chaw of tobacco. He had a slight paunch, expectorated a pale purple stream at frequent occasions, and managed to live up to all the horrible stereotypes of a Deep South state trooper

Fourteen miles we marched that day: twice as far as Sunday. At dusk we arrived at our second campsite, tramping in through the roustabouts and the Loaves and Fishes offerings and the latrine crew and the transportation crew, who were all out on the road applauding. We were dead tired, and it was hard not to cry. Everything was beautifully organized, compared to the first night. Supper lines formed immediately. This time, due to the distance from Selma, the food was rather cold chili beans in sauce, saltines, tomato section, fruit cup, bread.

Fowler and Rangel hit the sack immediately, but I strolled over to watch the entertainment provided for us on the bed of a truck. In spite of the many miles behind us and the miles to go, there was some of the most exuberant singing, dancing and guitar playing I've ever seen. I helped a bunch of kids get a fire started in an oil drum, and as I stood there warming the seat of my pants, Art Schriber of WINS, New York, appeared with a tape recorder. First he interviewed me for the network, and then recorded a message from me to Elizabeth, which he later played to her over the telephone!

I prowled over to the UPI truck and was treated to some bourbon and branch water by reporters Joe Holloway and Phil Sandlen. A joyous discovery on that evening.

A huge mob of clergy joined us that night in the tent that we had discovered the night before. About half an hour after we all bedded down, a man came in and ordered us out. It seems that he thought this was the press tent. No one paid the slightest attention to this would-be invader except one marvelously patient minister, who gently but firmly talked him out of his insanity.

Third Day: Tuesday, March 23

> Didn't it rain, chirrun
> Talkin' bout rain
> Oh, my Lord
> Didn't it
> Didn't it
> Didn't it oh, oh my Lord
> Didn't it rain?[2]

I awoke at 5:35 the next morning, and suddenly realized that my asthma was gone, and except for stiff legs and a slightly sore left foot, I was feeling better. I prowled around the campsite, taking pictures. Lost, alas.

As breakfast began, so did pouring rain. Ever prepared, I brought my expensive Haskell and Corthells' two-piece yellow slicker, and I put it on. Everyone else cut strips from the plastic ground sheets, made holes for their heads to poke through, and thus manufactured pretty efficient ponchos. I looked totally out of place.

Oatmeal and coffee, period, was what we were provided for breakfast, and spoons were in short supply. After breakfast I discovered a valuable secret: the cleanest latrines were

---

[2]Traditional spiritual, lyrics as sung by Mahalia Jackson, 1961.

the hardest to get to. Those on the trucks without hydraulic loading platforms involved a climb, rather than steps, and so were nearly unused. It is interesting how important this sort of thing becomes.

The three hundred marchers lined up efficiently, and this time George Fowler was in the first row while I was about five rows back. All that day I marched next to Mrs. Marie Foster, the secretary of the Dallas County Voters League. On her other side was Harris Wofford of the Peace Corps. Wofford and I took turns carrying Mrs. Foster's gear and offering her our arms for support. She needed help; on "Bloody Sunday" she had been clobbered by a trooper and had suffered a hairline fracture of her left knee. That night Wofford and I made a basket of our linked arms and carried her the last half mile into the tent, but the next day she was back in business.

Lining up had a slightly foreboding quality about it. The gloom of the weather and the prospect of "Big Swump" ahead were factors. A Reverend James Johnson from Selma offered an impassioned prayer calling on Jesus to protect us that day. He was a vastly dignified man, ageless, erect, carrying a heavy leather briefcase. Nobody smiled when, at the close of the prayer, he asked for divine guidance for " 'Martha Lou King" and "Reverend Abernickle." We all knew whom he meant.

It rained on and off all that day. I would get my rain gear on only to have the rain stop and the temperature go up. Then I baked for half a mile. As soon as I struggled out of the slicker, it would suddenly blast rain again.

The morning is a blur to me. The shacks and cattle of the day before gave way to mournful swampland, with much Spanish moss and occasional squashed water moccasins on the concrete road. Mrs. Foster said she had seen alligators. She also described the black community in Selma, and how about 20 percent of them did not approve of "The Movement." I wish I could remember all of her calm wisdom.

I met John Doar, the relaxed, capable number two man to Attorney General Nicholas Katzenbach, and also his assistant, Steve Pollock. Both were delighted with the way the march was going. Pollock said some of the troopers would never be the same again, having been impressed and moved by the spirit and good humor and the behavior of the marchers. I liked both of these men immensely. I was also impressed by LeRoy Collins, former governor of Florida, head of the Federal Community Relations Service under the Civil Rights Act.

Lunch took place on a high sandy bank, with rain spitting. Another WINS man sat next to me during the inevitable peanut butter. He told me Elizabeth had received my taped message late at night and had sent word back that all was well. A great relief! I had no idea whether she had made it back to Tuskegee, let alone Chatham Center!

The rain sped us along. My left foot developed a blister, and each rest stop made it feel worse. Everyone was tired and wet, so we stopped less and less. We got to our third campsite around 2 P.M. and discovered that the roustabouts had done their best in the midst of the muck and mire.

The mud was six inches deep. No trucks could get in or out, so they had only erected two tents, the largest ones. There were no plastic groundsheets, only home-made ponchos. A lot of stale hay had been spread, and it helped, but there wasn't much room for anyone. It was clearly going to be a rough night.

Fowler, Rangel and I spread out on one edge of the men's tent and rested while freedom songs and much coming and going swirled around us. I was interviewed by a correspondent for a Springfield, Massachusetts, radio station, a young woman named Juanita who looked about sixteen. I found out that she had nine children: four of her own and five foster children. I began to wonder if my mind was cracking up.

The next day I learned that one of the white ministers did go around the bend that night, suffering from paranoia. He was taken to Montgomery, where he refused treatment from anyone but a black doctor. They finally produced one, but when the minister discovered the physician came from New Jersey, he refused treatment. As far as I know, this was the only one of the three hundred marchers who dropped out.

Loaves and Fishes arrived about five. I had carefully "G-2ed the situation" beforehand and got Rangel out to stand where I was sure the line would be. To my dismay the line went elsewhere, and he needled me as we both hobbled to where it was. We were like a couple of lame old men, jabbing good naturedly at each other.

Supper was pork and beans with spiced tea. I finally decided I wanted a hamburger and a glass of Schlitz, so I drove into town with Fred Bennette, Mrs. Suarez of the Atlanta office of SCLC, and Ben Owen. Fred gave me the idea on the way that SCLC should have a working office in New York that might be involved in education programs.

I wanted to call home, so we went to the main office of the Montgomery Improvement Association, twenty-two miles from camp. It was awash with people, there to organize the black community to turn out to greet the marchers on Thursday. There was only one phone, which Bennette tried to commandeer for me. I got really sore and walked out in a huff. Then I took special pains to explain to them how important it was for me not to receive any preferential treatment. I think they all understood.

From there we all went to Bennette's room at the Ben Moore Hotel. This is quite close to the Capitol and was headquarters for the original Montgomery Bus Boycott. It is a shabby place, with sheet tin bedsteads, dreary wooden chairs, cracked plaster and broken Coke bottles in the halls. I sat in Fred's room and tried for a long time to call Elizabeth (circuits busy, etc.) When I finally got through she was out at the movies. After supper we decided it would be a nice idea to bring some Jack Daniels back to Fowler and Rangel. For a while we prowled the main black section, but there were no liquor stores to be found. So then we looped up past the Governor's Mansion and towards the State Capitol. All of a sudden we realized we were being followed closely by a "one-eyed" car. Other cars, loaded with white men, would pull up level with us, staring threats through the car windows.

At last we found a state liquor store, with "white" and "colored" entrances—it was closed! By then we all felt that the camp was the safest place to be, so we made tracks—within the speed limit.

On the way "home," Bennette and I discussed the concept of non-violence—how it was done in practice and how effective it is. He is a big rugged guy who obviously must have had to exercise great restraint in a situation like Bloody Sunday. He said it is much easier to suffer a beating yourself than it is to watch others getting one.

Non-violent resistance is, of course, the central device used by SCLC to reach its goals. The sit-in; filling the jails with willing, cheerful violators; answering hatred with love: these are the tools that can effect change.

Those methods have worked over and over again, but are most effective against bad laws or customs that institutionalize segregation, like the segregated rest room or the arbitrarily denied ballot. As soon as you cross the line into a system that honestly judges people on merit, non-violent protest—or any protest, for that matter—is self-defeating.

Take a specific example: Local 28 of the Sheet Metal Workers, AFL-CIO, used to allow only sons of members to qualify for apprenticeships. A sit-in to publicize this fact is effective, especially if coupled with a legal proceeding before the State Commission for Human Rights. But when the battle is won, and NYU administers a fair and impartial qualifying test and no Black man or woman passes, then the black protest "movement" takes a real beating if it calls a sit-in. The remedy at this point calls for an educational program, to qualify the young people being tested and to convince them that it is worthwhile.

I was in a very sobered state when we got back to the camp that night. For the first time in my life I had experienced the fear and the lonely hatred that is the lot of the southern Black. It took me a long time to get to sleep in the men's tent, where every square inch was filled (Fowler had kindly saved me a spot), and where once in a while an adolescent's changing voice would cry out in a dream. As I sat there in my muddy sleeping bag, rubbing my familiar charley horse and still tasting the fear of the road, I heard a kid shout "Give me the money, Willie!"

Fourth Day: Wednesday, March 26

I woke at 5:30 the next morning. A beautiful mist was rising from the fields, with soldiers of the 82nd Airborne cut off from the waist down by the watery illusion. Everything from then on had a greatly heightened importance and immediacy. After the night before, I knew more about what it was to be a Black.

Everyone seemed to be in a tearing hurry. I got into my mud-caked shoes and raced right to Loaves and Fishes, where I gorged on Special K.

We lined up haphazardly and stepped off on the road a few minutes before seven. Many people were still eating or using the john as we left. About three hundred yards from where we started, the road became four lanes again. I was in a line of three, next to a Selma woman with such an extreme southern accent that I couldn't understand her name or anything she said. She conversed with me enthusiastically during the morning, and I found it didn't matter whether I said "yes" or "how terrible." We got along fine. On her other side was a teenaged boy who would hardly talk at all. Fortunately, Mrs. Foster was right behind us with George Fowler, so there was plenty of support.

It soon began to get very hot, and we gradually peeled down, slathering our faces with heavy zinc oxide to fend off the rising sun just ahead.

Back on the four lanes—back to civilization. The wretched shacks began appearing again. A billboard had a huge picture of Dr. King, purporting to show him at a "Communist Training School."

The heat gradually got my left foot. In spite of the fact that I had a good pair of well-broken-in walking shoes, and a brand new pair of woolen socks plus foot powder every day, at lunch time I had to report to the first aid truck with a most impressive blister. A quiet northern White doctor slapped on a monstrous bunion patch, a soft pad with a hole cut to fit. It did wonders.

Dr. King arrived back from Cleveland shortly before the lunch break. It was quite astonishing how everyone's spirits perked up as he rejoined us.

All that day, from the time we got back on the four-lane road, we were met by streams of people coming out from Montgomery to join the march. The standard behavior was to disgorge enthusiastically from a charter bus in the south lanes, walk across the grass divider, and stand glowing and applauding as the line went past, and then either to retreat in humility to the end of the line, or to slyly and self-righteously scramble to the front, or at least as far front as the people already there would allow.

Some of the most aggressive line crashers were clergy-men. It seemed that the more resplendent the clerical garb, the more aggressive the man. It didn't matter what color they were, but you could tell in advance how far up front a man would land by the size of the crucifix on the chest. Those with the largest crucifixes usually made their way to the second or third rows.

It was interesting how our resentment rose at these new-comers. No matter how humble, appreciative and deserving the new arrival, he was entitled only to scorn or condescen-sion, and it took a real effort of will to remember that we ourselves must look a bit like gate-crashers to the Bloody Sunday veterans and the other SCLC regulars. It took an hour for our ranks to pass Montgomery Airport and then we moved past handsome modern industrial park developments. The all-white staffs of these places came out to stare at us.

Southern white bystanders divided up into several clear-cut types. The majority were the sullen but curious Starers. A sub-phylum of this class were the Wisecrackers. These were almost all younger men, and included those who made remarks about the nun's chastity and Leatherer's left leg. A small group got mad and shouted. These were both men and women, and were almost all older. The saddest of all, mostly younger women, were the ones who refused to look at all. They would turn their backs or hide their eyes as they went past in cars.

We marched through two brief rain showers, with enough sun and heat in between to dry off completely. The first took place on a long curving bridge over a railroad, from which we could look back at the lengthening line of several thousand people. Slack Johnson returned during this storm. George and I got separated from Rangel; for a while he was so far up ahead of us that we began to refer to him as "Bishop Rangel."

After the rain we pulled over to the side for what turned out to be the last rest stop of the entire march. Fowler walked up and asked Andy Young if I could walk with Dr. King for a while. We had discussed the idea of a Northern Christian Leadership Conference, and we figured that there would be no chance to talk to him the next day. Young and Dr. King agreed and, to the dismay of the ecclesiastical wolf pack, when the lines re-formed the front row consisted of George Fowler, Mrs. King, Dr. King and me! (see photo p. 20)

As we stepped off I started right in urging him to consider staffing a New York City office of SCLC. We discussed the difference in emphasis that would be necessary, and suggested that the focus should be educational rather than non-violent resistance to the law. The key as I saw it was to bring to such an educational program the same spiritual quality that they were showing in the March.

He didn't dismiss it, of course, but he hedged. The South is still the main arena for SCLC. Yes, I said, but look ahead. There are still more Blacks in New York State than in any other state, and their main problem is one of competition in a technological society. And then the rain began again, slanting down from behind our left shoulders. And as we marched across the Montgomery city limits, the line burst forth with "We Have Overcome!" Photographers were going wild and I was weeping and then the old Baptist hymns began, led by a magnificent big minister in the second row. I didn't know the words, but roared them out anyway as we passed a huge motel with balconies crowded with white people cheering the rain and laughing at us.

Even in the first row I had to fight for my place. A minister right behind me tried deftly to elbow me aside so he could walk next to Dr. King. I called on the civil rights song "We Shall Not Be Moved" for my inspiration, and stayed where I was. To my surprise, he gave up without trying to shove Mrs. King out of the way.

Finally, as the rain was letting up, Reverend Abernathy appeared with his wife and two small children, and I yielded my slot to them. Fowler was already back with the "bishop." I ran up to Andy Young to thank him for arranging my short audience, and then I suddenly realized how bad my feet were feeling. I dropped back with Fowler and Johnson and Rangel and we took our time, limping and allowing the fresh troops to swirl around us. By the time we arrived at the City of St. Jude, a Catholic school and hospital, we were far back in the pack. I think we realized that everything from here on would be a let-down, but we were determined to finish the last four miles the next day.

The last campsite was pretty muddy, and it had all the same equipment as the others, but it must also have had about fifteen thousand people milling around. We found our usual sanctuary in the press tent.

Slack Johnson had arranged with the brass at Alabama State University for us to come and have a shower. This is an all-black college, supported by the State of Alabama. We drove several miles through the black section to get there. I sat in the back seat this time, hunched down, and without fear. We were taken to the gym, where the basketball team was eating at their training table. We took our time under the hot water. What a wonderful feeling after five days! I called Elizabeth and found that all was well, and then we went out to an enormous T-bone steak dinner. A huge variety show featuring Harry Belafonte, Mahalia Jackson, Joan Baez, Nipsy Russell and Peter, Paul and Mary, was scheduled for 3 P.M. When we arrived back at the camp, there must have been thirty thousand people trying to get near the temporary bandstand. People in the front rows were fainting and being passed over the heads of the others to the stage, as they had been at the March on Washington in 1963.

At 9:15 the show hadn't started and I gave up. George and Charlie and Ben Owen were all back at the press tent, and we all sacked out. Soon the show started, and we could hear the acts from our air mattresses anyway. Sleep got me long before it was over.

We were awakened around 2:30 A.M. by a security man who said with much urgency and anxiety that a girl's jaw had been broken by a white agitator, and that our tent could not be protected because it was not under the light. With much grumbling we turned out and lay down near the communications truck. Then it began to rain.

Fifth Day: Thursday, March 27

For the first time since the march began, I woke up tired. There was a real mob scene on the field. At breakfast we realized that while we were at 'Bama State the night before, neon-red sleeveless jackets had been issued to all those who had marched the whole way. Without these, we were nobody. And all three hundred had been issued!

It took the next five hours for us to line up. Thanks once again to Andy Young, the twenty or so people who had not been issued their rightful jackets got them, and with much relief we stepped into line. Shortly after this, a group of us caught a Baptist minister trying to bribe one of the kids with a jacket to give it to him for fifty cents! We all made a big stink, which chased the minister away. A boy in line behind me asked me what all the fuss was about. When I told him, he said with a straight face, "They were paying three dollars last night."

At one point we ran into Abe Beame, the city comptroller of New York. In my mud-soaked clothes, sou'wester hat, bloodshot eyes and zinc oxide nose, he didn't recognize me!

Once again, George Fowler and I flanked Mrs. Foster. We were in the third line of those in jackets. The "bishop" was ahead of us, of course. It rained. People chanted, "Let's Go, Let's Go!"

Finally, after several false starts, we were met at the main gate by all the big brass, including Bunche and other well-known black leaders including Roy Wilkins, Whitney Young, and Phil Randolph. We all stepped off at about 11:00.

The last four miles of the march went through the poorest shantytown area of Montgomery. Wooden shacks with tin roofs with lines of little black girls dressed to the teeth with braids and wide eyes standing in front of wooden shacks with tin roofs. Gangly, skinny old women clapping slowly and chanting:

What do you want? FREEDOM!
When do you want it? NOW!
How much do you want? ALL OF IT!
Join the line! Join the line! Join us! On to the Capitol!

Then suddenly the people on the side for half a block were poor whites. Sullen, they stared from their porches as the marchers passed by. It took thirty thousand people an hour and a half to pass any one spot.

Then the street broadened out into a long downhill approach to the main business section. Here were lines of wise-cracking young white businessmen. Beauticians and their clientele looked out between slats of Venetian blinds.

Way up high in a hotel, a distinguished-looking sixty-year-old man leaned out a window, thumbing his nose at the march. We roared up at him, "WE LOVE YOU, COME JOIN US!"

We had started out eight abreast and, as usual, had to fight to keep our places in our lines, even with our red jackets as identification. Then we began to spread out, first to sixteen, then to thirty-two abreast. Each of us had either a small or a huge American flag. We passed a pretty square with a fountain, and then there we were on Dexter Avenue, sweeping beautifully one hundred yards wide and half a mile long up to the classic, columned portico of the Alabama State Capitol. From the pole over the dome floated two flags: the red and white Alabama emblem, and, above it, the Stars and Bars of the Confederacy. It was 1965, but the chosen flag was from another century.

We kept our line of march as far as we could go towards the steps where the blue line of the Alabama state highway patrol kept us from going any further to see Governor Wallace. And then we stopped.

We had walked fifty-four miles. As I leaned over to kiss Mrs. Foster goodbye, tears rolling off the zinc oxide on my cheeks, I remembered what someone had said the first day of the march: "When the greatest thing in our time was going on, where was your body?"

Mine was there.

5

Honored with Deep Roots

Right before I was born in 1928, my father, Winthrop Aldrich, was named president and board chairman of the Chase National Bank. This was after Chase Bank's merger with the much larger Equitable Trust Company, a state-chartered bank in New York. My father was in charge of what was then the largest bank in the world.

My mother, Harriet Alexander Aldrich, was known as a powerful, energetic social leader in New York City, so much so that in 1941 Mayor Fiorello LaGuardia asked her to head up the Civilian Defense Volunteer Office for the whole city. She led that effort throughout the entire war, while my father ran the efforts of Allied War Relief.

Always active in Republican politics, my father led fundraising efforts in New York for Alfred M. Landon (1936), Wendell Willkie (1940), Thomas E. Dewey (1944 and 1948) and Dwight "Ike" Eisenhower in their presidential campaigns. In 1952, as he retired from Chase, Ike appointed him ambassador to the Court of St. James's in London, and he served there for four exciting, transitional years, during the Suez Crisis as well as during the coronation of Queen Elizabeth II.

My paternal grandfather was no less imposing a character. Nelson Wilmarth Aldrich was born in 1841 to an impoverished family in Providence, Rhode Island. After the Civil War he successfully plunged into developing street

Photo taken of Harriet Aldrich, my mother, by unknown member of London press corps, and presented to her to honor her as one of their members. She was taking pictures beside them on the occasion of my father's coach ride to present his credentials to the Queen. They all adored her, and also admired her 3-D camera equipment.

railroads, connecting the region's small towns with Providence. He entered Republican politics at about the same time, where his forceful personality soon led him to dominate the Rhode Island Legislature. From there, it was an easy step to becoming senator from Rhode Island, a position that in those days was selected by the state legislature. He served in that capacity until 1912, and with canny and ruthless ambition and ability, became majority leader in the U.S. Senate during the administrations of Teddy Roosevelt and William Howard Taft. He was sometimes called "The General Manager of the Nation."

Grandfather's biggest test came after the Panic of 1907, when the Senate created the National Monetary Commission and Taft appointed him as its chairman. He spent the next five years studying the central banking agencies of all the major powers of Europe, often taking along his son, my father, Winthrop, on his trips to serve as his amanuensis. They collaborated on drafting a huge, comprehensive central banking law for the United States, but before it was adopted, Woodrow Wilson was elected president, and the National Banking Act of 1913 took their draft work and amended it, inserting a series of regional Federal Reserve banks to forestall the possibility of a single, strong federal bank.

The basic concept of that historic act was my grandfather's, and he died convinced that Wilson had stolen his thunder.

My father was the youngest of thirteen children, in an era when Americans tended to have lots of children so that some would survive childhood. Typical of that pre-penicillin era, five of his siblings died in childhood. Of the eight who survived, he was extremely close to four: Abby, Lucy, Richard and William. I cherish my memories of all of them.

Uncle Richard followed his father into politics in Providence, and for many years he was a congressman from Rhode Island. He was celebrated by his congressional peers as the most popular man in Congress. His wife, Janet, was superficially attractive, and they had one son, Dick, who as a young man was pretty hard for me to take. He was handsome, athletic, noisy, hugely confident, smoked cigars, and treated me with arrogant scorn whenever our paths crossed. This changed in later years after I had succeeded in the Police Department.

Dick had spent his early professional life in Sao Paolo, Brazil, working for the Rockefeller-sponsored International

Basic Economy Corporation (IBEC), learning fluent Portuguese, and marrying an adorable wife, Daisy Daggett. I liked them both so much by then that it was easy to forget the way I felt about him as a shy teenager.

When I ran for Congress in the 28th District, he was running in the 17th, on New York City's West Side. We were both beaten, which made our bond even closer.

So much has been written about my Aunt Abby Aldrich Rockefeller that I am reluctant to say much more other than a few personal remembrances. My father was twenty years younger that she was, and he was her greatest admirer. He once confided to me that his own mother had been "a vegetable for years," and that his sister Abby had been her substitute in his heart.

My earliest memories include a number of Christmas visits to her colossal, triplex apartment at 71 East Seventy-First Street in New York City. Dressed in my best, I would be escorted in by my father through a marble-lined reception room, and met immediately by his regal sister. She would then usher us into a huge adjoining hall, in which were hanging the enormous and imposing "Unicorn Tapestries," which Uncle John (Abby's husband, John D. Rockefeller, Jr.) had purchased from the Rochefoucald estate, and later gave to the Metropolitan Museum of Art. Dated from around 1500 A.D., the huge, magnificent French Gothic tapestries were so impressive that even a boy of five was overwhelmed by their beauty. They now hang in splendor at the Metropolitan's Cloisters museum in Fort Tryon Park.

We would be ushered into Aunt Abby's living room overlooking Park Avenue where, with great ceremony, she would present me with my Christmas gift. It was always the same: inside the outer envelope was a second one and inside that was a folded paper with an oval hole in it. Inside the hole was an engraved portrait of Abraham Lincoln. It was a five dollar bill!

I would thank Aunt Abby with great enthusiasm, and then she would ask me what I intended to spend it on. Carefully coached by my father, I would cheerfully reply, "I will put it in my savings account at the Chase Bank!" It often occurred to me to suggest to her that maybe the amount could have been a little greater, but of course I didn't.

Aunt Abby and Uncle John had a summer home in Seal Harbor, Maine. Known as The Aerie, it had been erected by John D. Rockefeller, Sr., resembled an enormous hotel and boasted a vast Japanese Garden (which still exists) and a handsome bowling alley in its basement. Occasionally, my family would leave our own extravagant "cottage" in Islesboro (which was about one-fourth the size of The Aerie), and zoom over to Seal on the *Little Wayfarer* to have lunch with the Rockefellers.

On one of those occasions, after lunch, Uncle John invited my sisters and me to the bowling alley for a game of duckpins. To our astonishment, he urged each one of us to compete, and offered to serve as the pinboy! He peeled off his jacket, and in his rather formal shirtsleeves, proceeded to set up the pins, and carefully returned the balls to us after our rather amateurish efforts to bowl. We were quite awestricken at the sight of him!

The senator's oldest surviving daughter was Lucy Truman Aldrich, born in 1869, who suffered a deeply disabling disease, possibly typhoid, which left her almost completely deaf at the age of eighteen. Pretty, irrepressible, wealthy and tough, she spent her entire life collecting Asian art, ceramics, statuary, and costumes. On most of her trips she was accompanied by a trained nurse named Minnie McFadden, who was almost as intrepid as Lucy herself.

On one famous occasion, in 1923, Lucy and Minnie were kidnapped by Chinese bandits from a train near Beijing, and her kidnappers forced her to flee on mule-back for two days before the Chinese Army came to their rescue.

Lucy wrote a letter to her sister, Abby, after this event. A masterpiece of understatement, it was later published in *Harper's Magazine*. As she told her adventure, the rather dashing and daring leader of the bandits was very protective of her, and as the Chinese army closed in, he left her alone near a primitive village where he said his wife lived and would protect her. Lucy slept on the ground in the rain that night, and was taken in by the women of the village, dried off, and placed in a warm bed. The following day the bandit leader reappeared and said he would release her. Again they charged off together on a donkey, this time to a railhead where the army and a representative of Standard Oil were waiting. She was free, but incredibly, the bandit leader kept hanging around! In fact, she herself interceded in his behalf when the authorities wanted to punish him for his misbehavior.

In her letter, Lucy reports that the man had been young, strong and handsome. He also spoke perfect English. My theory is that, for the first time in her life, Aunt Lucy had *really* enjoyed herself, and if the adventure had lasted much longer, she would have become a mighty Chinese empress.

She was, of course, a legend in our family, and very much adored. When I was in college in the 1940s I began to take the opportunity to visit her from time to time in Providence, usually with my father, but occasionally by myself. Because of her deafness, she was very hard to chat with, but even so, she was always ready to poke fun at herself and the people around her.

She once told me about the impressive antique candlesticks that dominated her front hall at the time. They were covered with authentic ancient Japanese symbols, and she reported a conversation she had had about them with the curator of Far Eastern Art at the Rhode Island School of Design. He was, of course, a completely inscrutable Oriental gentleman who never smiled or showed emotion in her presence. With great pride, she showed him the candlesticks, told him what she had paid for them, and asked him to translate the inscription for her. He doubled over into helpless laughter.

When he had recovered his *sang-froid*, he translated, "Property of Standard Oil of New Jersey."

She treated the whole event as a huge joke on herself.

Not long after, Lucy died at the Aldrich family home in Providence. There followed an extraordinary occasion, when twenty Aldrich descendants convened to divide up her possessions among themselves. All the Rockefeller brothers were there, my sisters and I, my father, Dick Aldrich, and several other cousins. I am sure Aunt Lucy was looking on from heaven, enjoying every moment.

If Lucy was my favorite aunt, then William T. Aldrich was my favorite uncle. He was small, round and jolly as Santa Claus, and truly adored all of us as children, and on into our adult lives. He was married to a marvelously affectionate woman, Aunt Dorothea. While I was a student at MIT and Harvard I drove out to their comfortable Brookline home for Sunday dinner and a warm visit nearly every weekend. He had an impish, droll sense of humor, loved to play parlor games like anagrams, and was a truly expert sailor, painter and architect.

During the 1930's Uncle William was the commodore of the Eastern Yacht Club near Marblehead, Mass., the place where every Boston-area yachtsman kept his racing vessel. This meant that he had a fierce but loving rivalry with my father, who at the same time was commodore of the New York Yacht Club, with its clubhouse at Larchmont, New York. They would hold competing regattas, and even extended the rivalry to the uniforms, braid, hats and other ornamentations with which they bedecked themselves.

Both Uncle William and Aunt Dorothea were rebels of a sort, though they worked to maintain their social positions. Instead of enrolling at Harvard or Brown, Uncle William had gone to the Ecole des Beaux-Arts in Paris, which left him with a distinctly rakish demeanor. Aunt Dorothea was a fierce patroness of the Boston Symphony, and had a weekly lunch with her friends at the Somerset Club, but also loved nothing more than the occasional off-color joke, which she would then report to the same friends.

Her favorite one was about the great white sale at Jordan Marsh after World War II, when two old ladies had a huge order marked with the initials of their church: the First Unitarian Church of Kittery, Maine. I told her the tale; her eyes lit up, and she said "I can't wait to tell Mercer Howe!" Mercer was her best friend, who loved off-color jokes as much as she did.

My maternal first cousin, Charles S. Whitehouse, a diplomat and former Central Intelligence Agency official who was ambassador to Laos and Thailand in the 1970's, wrote in his own memoir.[1] "A trait which I believe we all received from the Alexander side of the family is a great sense of fun."

He continued, "One final thought about the Alexander family is that there is a very large painting of the square in front of the Plaza Hotel on a winter night in the Edwardian Room of the Plaza. It shows 4 West Fifty-Eighth Street very clearly. I have never seen a picture of the house taken from Fifth Avenue, but when Mr. Crocker gave my grandmother the house as a wedding present, the garden of the Vanderbilts' house on Fifty-Seventh Street was where Bergdorf Goodman now stands.

"Mrs. Alexander was typical of the mothers of her time and saw to it that her girls were ready for the life they were expected to lead. They all went to Miss Spence's School in New York and none of them went to college. They all spoke French well and passable German. They played golf and tennis very competently.

"They rode sidesaddle very well (Aunt Harriet even was taught how to drive a four-in-hand) and their knowledge of art, furniture, silver, architecture, French, English and American history was remarkable, proof of what you can learn without a college education. They played the piano and were good dancers. I am inclined to believe that they were more accomplished in their early twenties than most graduates of today's universities."

Nelson Aldrich, my grandfather, commissioned a genealogist to trace the Aldrich family tree, a copy of which still exists. It traces the family name back to David Aldrich, born in Derbyshire, England, who arrived in the Massachusetts Bay Colony in November 1631 on the ship *Lyon*, and settled

---

[1]Charles S. Whitehouse, *Then and Now* (Marshall, Va., 2001).

in Braintree. This first American Aldrich's own eleven children busily intermarried with many of the first families of the colony, and the genealogy is replete with many prominent names, including Elder William Brewster of the *Mayflower*, Captain Israel Morgan, Jonathan Truman, Roger Williams, the founder of the Providence Plantations, and the wonderfully named Bathsheba Tilestone, my favorite progenitor.

Not to be outdone by her husband's formidable ancestry, my mother, Harriet, was descended from Major William Ferguson of the Continental Artillery, one of the founding members of the Society of the Cincinnati. He was captured by the British in the Battle of Long Island, in a major skirmish near Flatbush, and spent four years in a prison ship in New York harbor. I am his direct descendant, and as such enjoy full hereditary membership in the Pennsylvania Society of the Cincinnati, the oldest military hereditary society in the United States.

My mother was also the granddaughter of Charles Crocker, the three-hundred-pound powerhouse who built the Central Pacific Railroad east from Sacramento and across the Sierras to join up with the Union Pacific at Promontory Point, Utah, on May 10, 1869, creating the transcontinental railroad. His partners in this venture were Collis Potter Huntington, Mark Hopkins and Leland Stanford, and together they became known as "The Big Four."

My mother's father, Charles Beatty Alexander, held an honorary doctorate from Princeton, and traced his own ancestry through Archibald Alexander, a member of the Scottish Gordon clan who arrived in Philadelphia in 1737, and back to Robert the Bruce in 1245 and King Duncan I in 1034! I have always liked the idea that I am descended from warlike Scottish kings.

I had one older brother, Winthrop, Jr., who died in infancy before I was born, and I have four older sisters, Mary Homans, of Islesboro, Maine; Harriet Bering, of Winchester, Massachusetts; Lucy Burr, of Mystic, Connecticut; and Liberty Redmond, of Bethesda, Maryland. At this writing (2011) they all survive, except Mary Homans who died at ninety in Islesboro, Maine, in March of 2011.

6

Education

My parents chose the Buckley School on Seventy-Fourth Street in Manhattan as my primary school, and I walked the six blocks each day from our family home on Seventy-Eighth Street, accompanied by our butler or chauffeur or nurse. It was a rigorous academic program—a school for children of gifted parents—and doing well there almost guaranteed entry to the best prep schools and colleges in later life.

Weekends were spent at our family estate in Jericho, Long Island, guarded at night by private detectives—it was the era of the Lindbergh baby kidnapping—and summers were spent in Islesboro, Maine, safely out of the reach of polio and the baking heat of Long Island.

As children, we were certainly aware of the awful nature of the Great Depression, but never experienced its horrors, other than observing the sad, poor people rooting through the Flushing Meadows Dump as we were driven past by our chauffeur.

I suffered a severe ear infection when I was ten, which led to a mastoidectomy that almost killed me. My parents decided to send me to the Institut Le Rosey in Switzerland, where the altitude might have cured my asthma, but the threatened arrival of Hitler persuaded them to keep me in this country. They sent me instead to the Fountain Valley School in Colorado Springs, where I studied and grew and

Author at 17, the year I left St. Paul's School and started at MIT. By now, I was "Sam."

recovered my strength for two years. One of my most vivid memories is the Japanese attack on Pearl Harbor while I was at Fountain Valley. I returned east in the spring of 1942 and enrolled in St. Mark's Summer School, which my parents believed would be good preparation for entering New England's St. Paul's School, then considered the Eton of America's foremost boarding schools. I took a rigorous (and much appreciated) course in auto mechanics, and worked every day on nearby corn farms, weeding. It was wartime, and everyone worked hard.

St. Paul's was a shock after the easy-going atmosphere of Fountain Valley. The academic work was very demanding, the competition tough, and students had to compete in team sports, conducted in house leagues according to one's ability—football in the fall, ice hockey in the winter, and either baseball or crew in the spring. I still perceived myself as frail and weak, but there was no way out. It was "sink or swim!"

During my three years at St. Paul's, I maintained a respectable 80 average, and ended up on the fourth Delphian football team, the third Delphian hockey team, and the fourth Halcyon crew as bow man. I tried hard, but wasn't big or strong enough to be an athlete. I was musically inclined, sang in the choir, and taught myself the saxophone and clarinet well enough to play in the school marching band and also the Rubber Band, an embarrassingly bad musical group that played for the occasional school dances.

Although I made a few wonderful friends at St. Paul's, most of the time I was lonely, unhappy and homesick. I worked just hard enough to get onto the honor roll, but except for choir and the Rubber Band there was no activity I really enjoyed. I was still puny, sickly and neurotic, and worried about the prospect of being drafted into an all-consuming world war on my eighteenth birthday.

My father was almost as worried about my prospects in the military as I was. The specter of the final defense of Berlin and Honshu Island looked like a real bloodbath, with predictions of millions of Americans being sacrificed to achieve final surrender. Our fear was put into alarming perspective in December of 1944 when my first cousin, George Whitehouse, twenty-one, was shot down and killed over Luzon in the Philippines. I bore enough physical resemblance to him that my Aunt Mary would be consumed by racking sobs whenever she saw me.

I was fortunate in one area, I now realize. The excellent training I had received at Buckley prepared me to accelerate in virtually all academic areas. I was so advanced in French that I was able to complete all the offered courses by the end of my sophomore year. St. Paul's had to invent more courses for me and another former Buckley student, my friend David

McGovern. I requested a course on military French, and to this day I remember that a machine gunner is known as a *mitrailleur*. (We used to speculate whether a female gunner would be called a *mitrailleuse*.) I also recall that the largest French submarine was named *Surcouf*, and was equipped with a small floatplane, carried in a hangar just aft of its conning tower.

We also volunteered for a course in elementary Italian. At the time, the Tenth Mountain Division was grinding its way up the Apennines in Italy, and so we thought the language might be useful to us quite soon. I still recall the phrase *"Dove il gabineto?"* (Where is the men's room?"). Useful after the war's end, perhaps.

Mathematics was another area in which I had a head start, and not just from Buckley's superb grounding. One summer in Maine I persuaded Lester Hale, the Islesboro High School math teacher, to tutor me in advanced algebra and trigonometry. Hale was also the island's trash collector, and was pleased to have the extra pay. We worked each morning, and he left me with an assignment for the following day. The textbook got increasingly difficult as the summer wore on, but both Mr. Hale and I were patient and dogged about the work. When I returned to St. Paul's in the fall I passed the test in advanced algebra and trig, clearing the way for me to qualify for college the following year, a full year ahead of my graduating class. By the end of my fifth form (junior) year, in the spring of 1945, I had completed all of my high school requirements except sixth form English.

Pa decided that I should try to get a year or two of college under my belt, so I might qualify for some intellectual assignment such as being an intelligence officer. The problem of a sixth form English requirement seemed to become, in his mind and my own, a challenge to be overcome rather than a disqualification.

Happily, my sister Harriet had recently studied at the former all-male bastion of Massachusetts Institute of Technology, and that great institution was interested in attracting bright seventeen-year-old students who could pay tuition and who were interested in an accelerated degree program. A simple phone call determined that MIT was not in the least troubled by my lack of a high school diploma or sixth form English. Moreover, officials there remembered and liked Harriet. I began my studies at MIT in June 1945.

I spent my freshman year and the first half of my sophomore year at MIT, which was one of the most exciting places in America during the war. The atomic bomb was being developed, as was radar, and these and other wartime products were invented or being improved by the faculty of this enormous, Greek revival pile of masonry on the banks of the Charles River, opposite Boston's Back Bay.

In addition to the normal heavy science and engineering courseload, I enrolled in the Army ROTC program and was soon marching around the campus performing basic drill exercises. I fully expected to be drafted before the end of the summer of 1945, to find myself in the invasion of the Japanese mainland, where the American army expected to suffer at least one million casualties. This truly unreal eventuality was avoided by the appalling and unexpected leadership of President Harry Truman, whose decision to use the atomic bomb resulted in the end of the war in August, less than three months after I had begun my freshman year. In later years, when I heard people abhor that decision, I pointed out that it was likely the only reason I survived to listen to their opinion.

The Institute made one concession to social and personal mental health, which assuaged the general feeling of dead-serious intellectual effort: it offered a well-established fraternity system. Harriet maintained that only one frat—Delta Psi, known locally as the No. 6 Club, from its former address at posh Number 6 Louisburg Square on Beacon Hill—was worth joining.

I went to a couple of "mixers" at the No. 6 Club, designed to determine one's capacity for hard liquor, and was quickly invited to join. I became a new resident of the club, located on Memorial Drive near the MIT campus. I participated in the intense fraternal atmosphere, nightly study sessions, excellent breakfasts prepared by Allston, the steward, and the occasional explosive weekend parties. At one of those, a particularly capable science classmate invented a new martini cocktail, of 183 parts gin to one part vermouth, prepared in a laboratory beaker.

My closest friend at No. 6 was a tall, gawky sousaphone player from the Rubber Band at St. Paul's, Dudley Rochester.

Life at No. 6 was heavily programmed. Classes lasted all day, and late afternoon was occupied by an hour of intense card playing. The game of choice was no-stakes bridge, which I learned in a hurry. Out in the hall a splendid set of pool tables—both pocket pool and billiards—were in constant use. Supper was served by the club's steward, an amiable black man who looked after the "brothers" like a mother hen. After supper we retreated to our bedrooms, where we attacked the huge pile of homework we had been assigned. Around 11 P.M. we gathered again, trooping across the field near the club to the Howard Johnson's for a hamburger and a chocolate frappe. We ambled back to the club and went to bed exhausted.

Weekends were devoted to whatever social life Boston and Cambridge could supply, which was usually ample. Sometimes a local classmate would invite me for a swim at his home, or we went to the Totem Pole in Newton, a huge, liquor-free dance hall where it was sometimes possible to make friends with a girl.

I have very few memories of that first summer at MIT, beyond the fact that it was one of the hottest summers there on record, and air conditioning had yet to become widespread. I was seldom outside except for ROTC drills which, surprisingly, I found enjoyable. We wore simple khaki uniforms, with garrison caps that were indistinguishable from ordinary U.S. Army issue except that they had no added piping to indicate an assigned unit. I became sergeant, permitted to command maneuvers for a squad of six men, and later for several squads. From my coxswain days at St. Paul's I had a loud, deep voice, and it helped.

I was in Cambridge on August 15, for the celebration of the end of the war. My friends and I put on our uniforms and headed straight for the Boston Common, which was Boston's equivalent of Times Square. A delirious crowd of merrymakers had already descended on it, including hordes of young women intend on kissing servicemen. I am sorry to report that women we would have wanted to kiss stayed as far from the Common as they could. The women who did appear came in groups, often escorted by their own servicemen, who knew well that a kid with no piping on his cap was an R.O.T.C. nerd, undeserving of romantic compensation. We trudged back to the subway unkissed but happy, and decidedly relieved about the end of the war. We had participated in a historic occasion, hadn't been arrested, and felt quite proud of ourselves.

One problem then became increasingly clear: the principal reason I had enrolled at MIT had vanished, and I now had to confront the question: did I really want to be a physicist or engineer? What was my lifetime ambition?

I had asked the admissions office at Harvard if they would take me the following fall. They were only moderately disposed to do so, but finally said they would if I continued into my sophomore year at MIT, and I would have to start in the freshman year at Harvard without advanced standing. Harvard was always pretty stuffy about giving credit for academic work done elsewhere, even at MIT.

I declared my academic major in physics that winter at MIT. The work continued to be purely science and engineering, with no liberal arts or other creative work, and although the war was over the pressure to grind hadn't let up at all. I stiffened in my resolve to leave MIT at the end of the spring semester. By June 1946 I had successfully completed one and a half years of pure science at MIT, and I was ready to begin a whole new life. I had the satisfaction of being invited back to St. Paul's to attend my graduation with my class and to receive my diploma. The school had accepted my freshman English course at MIT as the equivalent of sixth form English.

It was at that ceremony that one of those "watershed moments" happened in my life. The commencement speaker was the father of one of the boys in the class. He was brief and to the point.

"Whenever in your life you have a choice," he said, "take a good look at the alternatives, and pick the more difficult one."

Robert Frost said it better:

> Two roads met in a wood, and I,
> I took the one less traveled by,
> And that has made all the difference.

I got a job that summer through Edgar Bering, my new brother-in-law, as a ranch hand on the Flying R Ranch in Mack's Inn, Idaho. It was a summer range for King Ranch cattle, owned by a Pocatello banker, and operated by a classic cowhand out of West Yellowstone, Montana. I learned to string barbed wire by the mile, and occasionally to herd cattle from one pasture to another along the highway. While the foreman and the other cowhand got to drive the main herd of six hundred cattle, I was entrusted with a smaller herd of about twenty-five "cripples," cows that were sick or had become entangled in wire and were limping.

One day I was shooing along my group of cripples when a car with Jersey plates screeched to a stop behind me, and a family leaped out and asked if they could take pictures of "a real cowboy." I cheerfully obliged, taking one of the children up into my western saddle with me. The family asked where they should send copies of the photos, and I gave them my New York City address. Their faces fell as they realized I was an urban cowboy, if that. I did discover one new skill that summer. From time to time a steer would get cut on a nail or wire: the foreman would rope the animal and we would lay it down to close the wound. While the other two held the animal down, I applied the needle and thread, and I wasn't squeamish about it.

Returning to Islesboro in time for Labor Day, I was sunburned, tougher, and quite ready to start at Harvard the next week. I felt grizzled, with a year and a half of college under my belt, and two months of real ranch work. For the first time I felt equal to whatever might come.

Four years at Harvard came next, and I found myself in the same class I would have been in had I stayed on at St. Paul's, but with several huge advantages. For one, I already had a year and a half of college and knew my way around Boston and Cambridge. Also, I had satisfied my science, math and language requirements, so I was able to tailor my academic program to courses I really wanted to study.

Harvard in the fall of 1946 was extraordinary. The normal freshman class had a thousand students, but that fall, with veterans returning to college and the GI Bill covering tuition, the college took in two thousand men, many of them five years older than the typical eighteen-year-old freshman. One large group consisted of members of the Tenth Mountain Division who had fought their way up the Italian peninsula during the war, although I didn't know any of these men until I met them at reunions many years later. Dormitory rooms had double-decker bunk beds in them, and students were packed in like sardines.

Academically, I decided to concentrate in American history and government. My faculty advisor turned out to be the great American naval historian, Samuel Eliot Morison, author of *Admiral of the Ocean Sea, the Life of Christopher Columbus*, and also the eighteen-volume *United States Naval Operations in World War II*. He also had co-authored, with Henry Steele Commager, the principal American history text in use at that time for high school students. I took his course on American naval history, for which Morison required all students to wear a jacket and tie in class. He was a pompous, snobbish martinet, but I thrived under his tutelage and wrote a solid senior paper for him on the 1777 Penobscot Expedition.

At the end of my junior year, during the summer of 1946, two classmates, Amory Houghton, Jr. and Herbert

Pratt van Ingen, enrolled with me in the *Cours des Vacances* at the Université de Paris (Sorbonne). It was the only second language experience I had while in college and I thoroughly enjoyed it. Many years later, during the Selma March, I called on the schoolboy French I had learned that summer.

I opted for the crew squad for my Harvard athletics, trying out for manager, but the competition was intense. My experience at St. Paul's (and my light weight) qualified me to serve as the most available coxswain on the squad. Day after day during my freshman year I took a series of eight-oared crews out on the Charles River. In my sophomore year, by default, I became the coxswain of the JV 150-pound crew. As a junior, I was good enough to cox the JV heavyweights. Harvard "swept the river" that year at the Intercollegiate Sprint Regatta on Carnegie Lake in Syracuse, and we enjoyed an undefeated season until our Yale race, in which both the JV and the Varsity lost. By starving myself and rowing single sculls in my spare time, I trimmed himself down to 127 pounds, still too heavy to be a varsity coxswain for my senior year.

I was invited to join the Porcellian Club in my sophomore year, and the club members elected me deputy marshal—the undergraduate president—at the end of my junior year. George Plimpton was club secretary that same year. The Porcellian Club is perhaps the most distinguished of the final clubs at Harvard, and I was always very modest about the honor of my Porcellian office, saying only that it "entitled me to drive free on the Taconic State Parkway," which was, and still is, a toll-free highway.

Harvard's junior varsity hockey team was disbanded for lack of funds while I was enrolled, so a group of players who had not made the varsity team formed a team we called "The Ticklers." We designed a uniform with a huge feather on the chest. One player, Duke Sedgewick, who was a six foot five inch college football star, was particularly anxious for us to have ice time with other teams.

Duke would get on the phone, call the coaches of suburban Boston schools such as Saugus High, and would offer to scrimmage them in practice games. It was too tempting

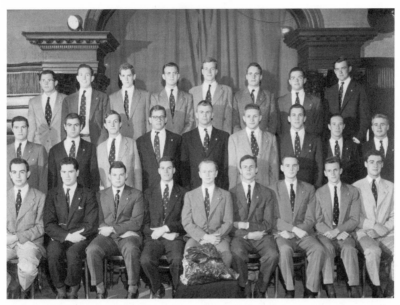

Official photo, Porcellian Club, 1950. Reading from left to right in the front row are Henry Gardiner, Albert B. Carter (from my crew), Harry Cabot, Arnold Hunnewell (librarian, and the best man at my wedding to Elizabeth), myself (deputy marshal), George Plimpton (secretary), Tarrant Cutler, David R. Carter, Charles Winn Gardiner. Directly behind me is Henry Dwight "Duke" Sedgwick, the hockey player, Edwin Upton Curtis Bohlen, my crew colleague, and C. Oliver Iselin, who accompanied me to Alaska. The boar's head at front center has been the symbol of the Club since 1791, and is made of china. The taking of these pictures is done annually by professionals, and they all hang in the club house at 1324 Massachusetts Avenue, Cambridge, Mass.

for the coaches to resist. At game time, Duke would be the first guy off our bus, with me, the substitute goalie, right behind him. We looked like Mutt and Jeff but, on the whole, our team played better than high school teams in the area. Duke hardly ever let anyone across the blue line, and a whole game once went by without my having to block a try on goal.

My health continued to be frail and problematic during my college years, and in December of my senior year I suffered a mild attack of what turned out to be polio. I wore a back brace for about a year, and forever after felt that the Lord had saved me for something better: I was medically barred from serving in the armed forces, which kept me out of the Korean War.

At roughly the same time, I was diagnosed with a duodenal ulcer. The infirmary prescribed a milk diet, and the resulting inflation to 180 pounds emphatically ended my coxing career. Instead, for the ensuing two academic years I coached the Elliot House crew to undefeated seasons.

Today, at the age of eighty, I still work out on rowing machines, imagining I am on the Charles River with the wind at my back, going past Eliot House on my way home to the Newell Boat House.

During the summer before my senior year, C. Oliver Iselin III, a Porcellian "brother," and I bought a used army ambulance and drove together to Alaska on the Alcan Highway. We accomplished nothing but still remain friends.

My final Harvard achievement was aceing the Law School Admissions Test (LSAT) in the spring of 1950. I scored in the upper first percentile on the test, which enabled good law schools around the country to consider me—in spite of my B and C+ grades.

In the summer of 1950 I went to Henley, England, with the Harvard Crew as their official photographer (at my own expense). Then a group of Harvard friends and I toured France and Italy together. On my return to the family estate in Islesboro, I got the news that I had been accepted at both the University of Pennsylvania Law School and Harvard Law School for the following semester. It was about that same time that I began squiring around Elizabeth Hollins, a beautiful nineteen-year old summer neighbor. I was twenty-three, and very much enamored of her.

Harvard Law School in 1950 was the single most competitive place in North America. Scott Turow's book, One L, only hints at the savage pressures that bear upon the school's students, not only from rapacious professors, but also from other students. It is often recounted that, during the 1930s, the dean addressed the first year class and asked each

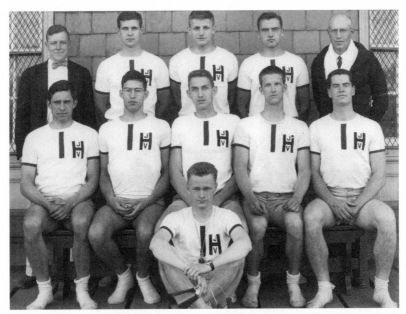

I am seated with my megaphone. The second row is framed by Bill Saltonstall (left) and Porcellian Club member Albert B. Carter (right). Behind Carter in the back row is our coach, Tom Bolles. To Bolles' left stands our stroke, Art Rouner, and to his left is Edwin Upton Curtis Bohlen, another Porcellian, who later enjoyed a fine career as an American diplomat. In front of Rouner and next to Carter sat Louis Cox, whose older brother Archibald, distinguished himself by resigning as Solicitor General during the Watergate scandal in 1974. Louie was slightly crosseyed, and was thus dubbed "Screwy Louie" by all his good friends on the Crew. Happily, that never prevented him from becoming a great Wall Street lawyer in later life.

man to look at students seated on both sides and realize that two of them would not be there the following year. By 1950 HLS had figured out that this was wasteful, and the school was trying to make it possible for all to survive, but that effort did nothing to abate the relentless pressure. I studied until the library closed, and then went back to my room and continued studying until I collapsed.

My life at Harvard College had not prepared me for the rigors required at Harvard Law. I tried to maintain a semblance of normalcy by rooming with a good friend from the Porcellian Club, Arnold W. Hunnewell Jr. I spent many weekends driving Route 20 to Smith College in Northampton, where Elizabeth was a freshman. I coached the Eliot House crew on weekday afternoons. While I was courting and crewing, the rest of the law school class went sailing right past me, academically.

Somehow I managed to survive, although among the bottom ten members of the class all three years. The only A grade I received was in my final year, in a course on equity taught by Zachariah Chafee. Before the final, I researched the latest cases in that arcane subject, found a few that were current and in conflict, and gambled that old Zach would ask about those cases. I aced that test, and received the A I had earned.

That spring I attended the Harvard commencement as an assistant marshal for Harrison Tweed, who was grand marshal. While sitting around the table in the Porcellian Club before the exercises, Mr. Tweed asked me to go to work at his firm, Milbank, Tweed in New York. As one of the ten "anchor men" in the law school class, I was grossly unqualified for the job, but against my better judgment I said yes. It turned out to be foolish, both for him to offer and for me to accept.

There is one remaining event in my education, and it doesn't belong here! After I had cut my childhood ties with the family, I began a wonderfully adult effort to school myself in the profession I had selected: public administration. I began the process while working in the field as a deputy police commissioner, by enrolling at the New York University School of Public Administration and Social Services at Washington Square. It was a tough, demanding night school, staffed with expert city government officials, filled with able students eager to rise in government positions. I am proud to say I did very well there. I received my masters degree there in 1960, and was honored for the best thesis. The prize was a briefcase.

7

Marriage and Milbank

Elizabeth and I were married in August of 1951, after my first year at Harvard Law School. The ceremony was at Christ Church in Dark Harbor, Maine, attended by a large gang of our friends, including Eddie Auchincloss and Justine Eaton, who met there and later married and became our best friends in New York. David McGovern was my best man, but he was in Korea and Arnold Hunnewell filled in for him. We left the reception in *Little Wayfarer*, my family's boat, and the fog closed in over us as we steamed away. Our honeymoon was spent at the Pebble Beach Club in Monterey, California, where I tried rather unsuccessfully to teach Elizabeth how to play golf. I purchased a white 1951 Pontiac out there, and our honeymoon consisted of driving all the way back to New York, via Yellowstone Park, the Badlands of South Dakota, and a long series of deadly Midwestern towns where tourist accommodations were hard to find. It could have been a more auspicious start.

I went straight back to classes at HLS. We moved into 60 Brattle Street in Cambridge, not far from HLS and a subway ride from the Longy School of Music where Elizabeth enrolled to study piano. We lived as newlyweds there for what I thought were two happy years, Elizabeth studying the piano and writing poetry while I tried to study even harder than I had the preceding year when I was courting her and coaching crew.

I still ended up in the bottom ten of the class.

Elizabeth became pregnant late that winter, and so we planned to have a quiet summer in Islesboro, visiting with her mother, artist Ibbie Holmquist, and her stepfather, Goran. I took a summer job clerking for Alan L. Bird, Esq., in Rockland, where I was given "hopeless cases." I tried to make sense out of a tangled property title, a deadbeat creditor of his who turned out to be in jail, and a few other messes including the affairs of the Islesboro Inn—which I had to ask to have demolished—and the Tarratine Club—which was so close to bankruptcy that we had to go around the island begging other summer people to join. I ended up being president of that club that summer, because nobody else wanted the job.

Our first child, Elizabeth, was born in October, and we nicknamed her Ibbie after her grandmother. She was a radiant, loving creature, and I thought the world had turned into heaven. That spring I began to hit my stride in school a bit, getting that redeeming A in equity, and judging some of my younger associates in moot court competitions.

The following summer, with a job promised in New York, we began looking for a place to live. We both had strong families in Manhattan and apartments in Manhattan were beyond our means—Milbank paid new legal hires $4,000 a year—so we preferred to start our lives somewhere else. But neither of us wanted a commute. David Devens, my brother-in-law, recommended we look in Brooklyn Heights, one subway stop across the East River. I asked around Milbank and was referred to a Mrs. Darwin R. James, a client of the firm, who owned property there. I was able to buy a wreck of a house from Mrs. James on Columbia Heights, with a splendid view of Lower Manhattan, for $21,000. Both sets of parents thought we were out of our minds, but we forged ahead and never regretted the decision.

I worked at Milbank for three years, living happily in Brooklyn Heights and starting a wonderful family. Winthrop was born in February 1954; Amanda in November 1956 and Alexander in March 1958—each one adorable. We employed a series of Norwegian women au pairs who helped Elizabeth with endless diaper changes and other duties incident to her motherhood. She also continued with her poetry.

At the law firm, I tried mightily to find a niche without much success. The first year I was assigned to be an aide to "Pic" Bennett, an elderly securities attorney, who delegated to me the most tedious part of a bond issue financing for Abraham and Straus, the vast retail empire in Brooklyn. He assumed I knew everything I needed to know about the subject—which I did not—and I was immediately at sea in meaningless minutiae. I lasted in this morass for about a year, unhappily. The next fall the National Tax Reform Act of 1954 took effect, renumbering every provision of the code and changing it substantially. I figured it might be a good time for a young attorney to jump into the field. I also admired Weston Vernon, Jr., the senior tax attorney at Milbank, and asked if he would take me on as his clerk, and he did.

It didn't take me long to discover that tax law was even more dreary and tiresome than securities law. I began to spend more and more time on civic matters, such as the Brooklyn Academy of Music, the Brooklyn Institute of Arts and Sciences, the Brooklyn Association for Mental Health, The Heights Casino (a Brooklyn club that a group of us saved from bankruptcy), and the Parks Association of New York City. All of these worthy groups were lined up for me by the very same Mrs. James who had sold us our house.

I had been encouraged to do all these things by the firm, but it constantly interfered with the legal work I should have been doing. I found these civic matters to be much more to my liking than the number-crunching of tax laws. In the final endeavor, the Parks Association, I led an effort to prevent Larry Gerosa, the New York City comptroller, from selling parks land to private developers. This led to the landmark case: *Aldrich v. the City of New York,*which found that lands that had been acquired for parks use could not be alienated and sold to a private developer.[1] It did not occur to me then that I might have found a new career!

---

[1]208 Misc. 930, 939. "Aldrich v. City of New York, 208 Misc. 930, N.Y. Supp. 1955, Oct. 25, 1955." The appeal is "Aldrich v. City of New York, 154 N.YS.2d 427, N.Y. A.D. 2 Dept. Jul 9, 1956." We prevailed in both cases.

The law firm began to realize that I was ill-suited for the kind of legal work they did and, in the winter of 1955, I was assigned to work for a month at the New York City Legal Aid Society, serving as a volunteer attorney at the Magistrate's Court above the Tombs Prison on Center Street, representing indigent defendants in criminal proceedings.

I loved it! Every day for five weeks I represented up to twenty-five defendants at their arraignments, in cases ranging from narcotics possession to murder in the first degree. I quickly learned how to move for a dismissal when the evidence was insufficient, how to transfer the case to Bellevue Hospital for a psychiatric evaluation, and when to ask for a more experienced attorney from Legal Aid to step in when an angry judge became exasperated at my arguments. The week after I left that wonderful assignment, Eddie Auchincloss's Uncle Charlie asked me to attend a lunch hosted by the Prison Association of New York, to hear an address from the new city police commissioner, Steve Kennedy. I went, filled with curiosity. Kennedy was inspiring, spoke about his plans to reform the huge police bureaucracy. I listened with rapt attention. Then he asked for questions. No one responded.

With some trepidation, I put up my hand and asked him, "I have just served as a volunteer at Legal Aid, and I noticed that police personnel in Magistrate's Court often have to sit for hours and sometimes days for their cases to be called. Isn't this an awful waste of police time?"

Kennedy's face lit up, and he exclaimed, "That's a *really good question!*"

He went on to explain that he had tried for years to persuade the courts to address the problem, but that they were very slow about it. I went back to Milbank that day, and asked the firm to assign me to the litigation department, hoping it would ignite the same excitement in me that Legal Aid had. They did, but I soon found myself defending Bache and Co., whose reps had sold West Virginia Turnpike bonds to widows and orphans, despite knowing the bonds were worthless. The widows sued, and I had to defend the big heartless firm.

Just before Labor Day that same summer, Elizabeth and the children were in Islesboro and my bag was packed to join them, when the Milbank telephone operator called me and announced that Commissioner Kennedy was on the phone for me. He said he had a job to fill in the department and might I be interested? Could I come to headquarters that very afternoon to discuss it with him?

I told him I had tickets to fly out of LaGuardia that evening at eight, and he suggested I meet him at his office at five and he could give me a ride to the airport, since he lived very nearby and he was on his way home. Shaking like a leaf, I agreed.

My life was about to change forever.

I took the subway to police headquarters at 340 Centre Street, carrying my overnight bag. A kindly old cop leaned out of the enclosure that surrounded the desk and said, "Yes, kid?"

With as much composure as I could muster, I explained that I had a date with the commissioner. I was directed to an office on the remotest corner of the second floor, still carrying my bag. No security search or ID check.

Kennedy's office was large enough to hold conferences in, and featured a small antique desk in its center, originally belonging to Theodore Roosevelt when he had been chairman of the police commission three generations earlier. Kennedy was sitting there when I arrived, giving orders to someone on the phone.

He shook hands with me warmly and immediately reminded me of our first meeting at the Prison Association meeting. He knew quite a lot about my education and my job, and I guessed he had done some careful checking around before asking me to come to the office.

He told me that he had an empty job title in his departmental budget: secretary of the department, at an annual salary of $7,500. This munificent amount was about $500 more than I was then being paid, and it came with a car and a driver. It had been assigned to the department's public relations and press officer, who was now a deputy commissioner. Steve said he intended to change the position into a personal aide to the police commissioner, with an office near his at headquarters.

He drove me to LaGuardia Airport in his official car, with seven police radios chattering simultaneously from each borough headquarters. I decided during that drive I would take the job as soon as I spoke to my wife, Mr. Tweed at the firm, and then to my father.

By the time I talked to my father, both my wife and Mr. Tweed had approved the idea, and I never gave my father the chance to say no, which, of course, I knew he would have. I called the commissioner the following Monday and accepted his offer.

It was the most exhilarating thing I ever did. I had never enjoyed the law as practiced in the big New York firms; in fact, on one occasion, I had enrolled in an NYU-sponsored series of aptitude tests to find out what I was really suited for. They determined that I was most able to discharge the role of airline pilot: able to bear many hours of routine, interrupted by short bursts of sheer terror. My newly chosen career seemed destined to live up to this prescription.

The following four years served to demonstrate clearly to me that my rebellion was confirmed. It was in the Police Department that I found my career in public service.

8

On the Beat

My first day on the job as secretary to the New York City Police Department was also my introduction to the city police press. These were the newsmen who occupied a "shack" in an alley behind headquarters, and who had been on the job for years. They had a special, cynical approach to police work, believing that all police were corrupt, and the higher the rank, the worse they were. My appointment was a well-kept secret until the day I reported for work, October 15, 1956. I was ushered into the office of Walter Arm, deputy commissioner for community relations, formerly a reporter for the *Herald Tribune* assigned to the "shack." Before turning me loose, he gave me just one piece of advice: "Never let the bastards take a smiling picture of you. They will wait to use it until the day some poor kid is killed by a cop, and then they'll show you smiling like an idiot."

His feelings about the police press corps were every bit as cynical as the reporters' opinions of the police. The reporters had no information about me other than information from a news release saying I had been an attorney at Milbank, Tweed. The first question I was asked was: "Are you making a financial sacrifice to take this job, Mr. Aldrich?"

I had to think, trying to remember how much I was earning at Milbank, which had been about $5,000 a year. I paused, and told them, "No, not really. I'll be earning a bit more in this job."

1959 at Police Athletic League.

They were astonished to discover that lawyers at Milbank didn't earn as much as many of them. The *Daily News* headline the next day read, "Wall Street Lawyer Paid Less Than Police Secretary." A few days later those reporters found out I was Ambassador Winthrop Aldrich's son, and cousin to the Rockefellers. They were furious that Arm hadn't tipped them off. Both he and I felt my first contact with the press had been acceptable.

Commissioner Steve Kennedy was quick to give me assignments. "I want you to work on two jobs for me," he said. "First, you need to learn as fast as possible how this department operates. Get to know the other deputies and learn about their responsibilities. Visit every command in the field. Spend some time at the Police Academy. Visit some of the busiest detective squads. Ride with the emergency service division," he ordered. "Don't be a nuisance, but learn how things work, and let me know what you think. How are cops recruited and trained? Do we do an adequate job in screening our recruits? Keep your eyes and ears open, and your mouth closed."

Kennedy's second assignment for me was more concrete. "One of our worst problems is in the area of personnel selection. Now and then I need someone who has a unique skill to perform a special assignment, and unless I'm familiar with a cop with those skills, it is very difficult to find the right person."

He explained that sometimes he needed a man who speaks Spanish, who could operate a bulldozer, and who lived on Staten Island.

"We have a personnel records unit with a lot of expensive IBM machines, but they can't sort our personnel for these needs. I want you to develop whatever system it takes to make it possible," said the commissioner, advising me that Acting Captain Bill Hambrecht commanded the Personnel Records Unit (PRU), and that he would cooperate.

Those first two assignments took me a couple of years to complete. There were about twenty-four thousand policemen in one hundred precincts, and the same number of detective squads. There was a civilian clerical force of several thousand. The department had deputy commissioners for legal matters, community relations, administration, licenses, and the youth division. Directly under the commissioner was the chief inspector, in charge of the uniformed force, and a chief of detectives. There was a first deputy commissioner (also named Kennedy), and a myriad of special squads or commands, including narcotics, public morals, the police academy, and emergency service.

Two or three times a week I arranged to spend time with commanders of various sub-groups in the department, taking copious notes and learning the basics. The only person who seemed difficult toward me was the appropriately named deputy commissioner for administration, Martin H. Meaney, an older Irish politician nearing retirement, one of the "old guard." He and Steve Kennedy didn't like each other, but Meaney was too entrenched with the Roman Catholic Diocese of New York to be fired. Francis Cardinal Spellman, the archbishop, took a very parochial interest in the affairs of the department, and if Steve had moved to get rid of Meaney, the cardinal would have called the mayor the next morning.

So Meaney stayed on, running a number of offices and functions, including the print shop. Our paths would cross within a few short weeks, helping to define me within the department. Of course, nobody was more ignorant about police work than I was at the time. I attended classes at the Police Academy, including one in which a patient instructor taught me to shoot a .45 caliber pistol and then advised me never to pack one—not because I hadn't learned, but because I had too many children in the house. I sat in on departmental trials, served on selection boards for new cops, attended every staff meeting in the commissioner's office, and had frequent evening meetings with Steve himself. I took copious notes, and then destroyed some of them so I had to remember it all.

I spent a few days at the Division for Licenses, where everyone who worked in a bar, restaurant or other place that served liquor had to apply for clearance. There had once been a civilian commission that performed this task, but it had been so corrupt at some point in the dim past that the City had transferred the functions to the police department.

One day while I was there, the great comedian Jimmy Durante came in personally to renew his license. His nickname was "the schnozzola" in honor of his principal facial feature. I was introduced to him, and his only words to me were "DON'T TOUCH DA NOSE!"

The building that housed the license division was across town on Vesey Street, and was later razed to make way for the World Trade Center. It featured a flat wire basket suspended from a creaky pulley over a central indoor court. Old files were stored in a huge attic room, and were lowered down in the basket to the first floor when needed.

The division licensed a wide variety of vehicles and public places and jobs and functions, from public hacks and hack drivers to cabarets and dance halls, and covering "sound devices," including anything that sent blaring voices or music out to the public. The power to license implied the power to withhold a license, which the department took to mean that we had to investigate to see if applicants had a criminal record. Occasionally, as in the case of Gene Krupa, the world-renowned drummer, some were found to have a drug record, and were barred from performing in New York City.

I was very curious about the regulations for taxi drivers, especially those who refused to go to Brooklyn from Manhattan. I found that this was absolutely illegal, and was grounds for lifting the hack driver's license. The next time it happened to me, I simply mentioned that I had been license commissioner, and the driver folded up like a tent and took me to Brooklyn. One of my most challenging departmental tasks was to haunt and master the functions of the Personnel Records Unit (PRU), housed in the detective division across Spring Street from headquarters at 400 Broome Street. Staffed almost entirely by "limited duty" personnel whose "Guns Had Been Removed" (mostly men who had suffered either physical or psychological disability and had been declared unfit for regular police duty by a police surgeon), it was the office that contained all of the most modern computer equipment that was available in 1950. The entire roster of 24,000 men and women and all civilians assigned to the force had painstakingly been entered onto punch-card records. Rosters, payrolls, discipline records, constantly shifting assignments, name and address changes, injuries and deaths, marriages, and pension data for all members of the department were continuously being processed and massaged by this office. Huge card punchers, collators, printers and other processors developed by IBM were jammed together on one vast floor, which had to be air-conditioned, not for the humans in the building, but for the machines.

My most urgent job was to develop a system of identifying all the skills possessed by 24,000 people and a process for entering them into the PRU machinery. With Kennedy's help I assembled a five man team to do this job. Our goal was to be able to define the skills needed, and to write a one-page form for information to be transferred into punch cards. It took our team two months to come up with an effective system. We ended up with codes for sixty-five languages, including "other." I am glad we put that in, for we found we hadn't included Tagalog, Tonkinese, Hindu, Assamese, Bengali, Basque and Sign Language, for each of which the department already had staff speakers. We didn't stop there. Job skills were almost as useful as the languages. Many detective division assignments were "plants," and the ability to find and assign a detective with the ability to operate a bulldozer or a sheet-metal bender or to play a musical instrument might be crucial to the assignment.

Finally we designed the all-important one-page form that had to be filled in by all department employees. I had carefully arranged for the department's print shop to run off the necessary forms, about 35,000 of them. On the day the printers had promised to start, one of my team found that the supervisor had removed our forms from the printing machines and was printing pistol targets.

I took a very deep breath and asked myself, "What would my mother do?" The answer came through loud and clear: I threw an old-fashioned Presbyterian hissy-fit! I called the offending supervisor, ordered him to "putthosegoddamforms-backwheretheybelongedandneverpullanythinglikethatonme-again!" Two minutes later, his boss, Deputy Commissioner for Administration Martin H. Meaney, an old-line Irishman who had held his job since 1934, called me in a fury for calling one of his "people" without going through him first. I apologized to him for that lapse, and then asked him if he had authorized taking my forms off the machines, and he innocently denied it. I told him I would not tolerate bureaucratic delays and to let all his people know what a bastard I was. I immediately called Steve and told him about the interchange, and his response was, "Good for you!"

I guess I had earned my spurs with that event, for I never had any other trouble with my deputy commissioner colleagues, least of all Mr. Meaney.

The following Monday I asked for agenda time in the commissioner's weekly staff meeting. I wanted to show everyone the form and get their support in having all staff fill it out. As usual, we assembled on time, but before my agenda was reached, the commissioner's lieutenant aide came in and announced a huge explosion on the Brooklyn waterfront.

Kennedy immediately assembled all the deputies in a small fleet of cars. I was in his, and we all headed across the Brooklyn Bridge, surrounded by what seemed to be every piece of fire apparatus in Manhattan. As we drove past Brooklyn Borough Hall we observed that every window in it and the office buildings nearby had been shattered by the blast, which had occurred about a mile away!

Sirens screaming and lights twirling, our cars went straight to Thirty-Third Street on the Red Hook waterfront, the entrance for the longest pier in the Erie Basin. For more than a century the pier had been the southern terminus of the Erie Canal system. Billowing smoke filled the whole area. An enormous temporary structure containing a Salvation Army canteen already dominated the entrance, dispensing food and coffee and simple medical supplies. I expressed surprise, and was told by Steve that "the Army" was always the first to respond at any disaster, and fulfilled a crucial need, always well ahead of the Red Cross and any other aid organizations.

Ambulances were everywhere. We learned that nine people had been killed, and 247 injured. The fire was started by welders on the roof, whose sparks had ignited some flammable material on the floor of the pier. It was later reported that a huge stash of paint, ammunition and other explosive materials had been stockpiled there for later shipment, and it all went up at the same time. Fortunately for the fire and police personnel and others who were actually inside the pier building, the force of the blast went up and outwards in an arc. Many of the injured were on fireboats that were playing their hoses into the building when it blew up. They were blown into the water, but the men inside the building were not hurt.

Steve and I and my other colleagues were there all the rest of that day, working with him on communications with other departments, the mayor's office, and the press. When

I got home that night, I smelled so badly of smoke I needed two showers before going to a Brooklyn Heights party for the Rembrandt Club, an arts group. Even then, the fastidious members ganged up on me and sent me home. I smelled too bad.

The following week I was able to give my report and my form to the cabinet, and then came the next big test: presenting the program to the press.

The forms went out to every command, and in due course they were returned, punched in and assembled. Captain Bill Hambrecht, the leader of our team, selected a whole deck of all the language cards, and we got the police reporters from the "Shack" to assemble in the huge IBM room of the PRU. I asked them to tell me what to find.

"A Yiddish-speaking Irishman!" shouted one reporter.

"Aaronson, Aaronson, Aaronson" printed the computer.

"Keep going!" the reporters cheered.

"Abramowicz, Abramowicz, Abramowicz" came next.

And so it continued through the alphabet, up to the "M"s.

And then, among a forest of Jewish names, suddenly appeared MacShane, Frank, assigned to the Coney Island Precinct in Brooklyn. We sent a car out to the boardwalk to get him to call in, and within minutes we connected him with the reporter, who addressed him in Yiddish. To my enormous relief, Frank answered him in Yiddish. He also confirmed that he was, indeed, of Irish descent, but had always lived in a Yiddish neighborhood, and spoke the tongue fluently.

The *Daily News* ran a favorable article about the new police program. Steve Kennedy was happy.

One of any police commissioner's biggest challenges is any civilian complaint about police misconduct or brutality. Complaints happen frequently, sometimes when a person has to be subdued in order to effect an arrest, especially when the complainant is injured, and even more especially when police fire fifty shots into someone they are trying to subdue. Sadly, most reporters are likely to look for the "bad cop" in each story, and are often quick to believe the complaints of brutal arrests. A wise commissioner does well to avoid such an assumption, but to look instead at patterns of behavior on the part of the cops.

Steve Kennedy was a famously good cop, the first member of the department to attend the FBI Academy in Washington, with a very high record as a brave and effective cop and commander over his years of service. He stoutly maintained firm control over the handling of such complaints, and he was correct in so doing. He consistently resisted any efforts on the part of people who asserted that the only effective way of controlling the problem was by giving control of it to entirely civilian groups, with representation on those groups of every minority in the city. He believed that such a process would become politicized, and would lead to the police abandoning the unpleasant business of enforcing the law entirely. His answer to the problem was to keep the job firmly in the control of a tough and honest commissioner, his civilian deputies, and a few carefully selected, high-ranking officers. This was the way it was done when I arrived in 1956, and for the four years that followed.

After I had served a few months as secretary of the department, he carefully assigned me to sit on these boards, first as an observer, and then as a full voting member, and finally as chairman. The hearings were performed with full due process. The complaining civilians could be represented by counsel, but were afforded both respect and attention even if they were not. Stenographic notes were taken. A specially trained sergeant would provide the board with a full record of the officers charged in the case, including any prior record of similar behavior.

A typical board consisted of a full deputy commissioner, a deputy chief inspector, a precinct captain or desk lieutenant, and the investigating sergeant. A real effort was made to include on each board a representative of the racial or ethnic groups of the complainants, as well as at least one attorney.

Since a finding of probable cause in one of these cases could very well destroy a man's career, each board tended to apply a fairly high standard of proof on each complaint. This fact alone may have led to an appearance of favoritism toward a cop, but that could easily change if the sergeant's report showed a significant record of similar behavior in the past, or other serious disciplinary lapses.

As a general rule, I can say with some confidence that a finding of "no probable cause" was almost always in the interest of both the public and the department. Otherwise, the civilian had either proved his case, or the cop didn't deserve to be in the job. In either case, both cops and the public had confidence in the process once they knew how it was performed.

To the ACLU or more radical activist groups, having the police department investigate itself was outrageous. In my book, giving those groups a role in the process would have been disastrous. Take your pick!

I found the New York City judiciary fascinating: a study in Byzantine complexity. I could fill these pages with its organization table and its developmental history. One of its features was a separate parole commission for juvenile offenders, and it was specified that a high-ranking civilian representative from the police department should serve thereon. At some point during my learning curve, Kennedy selected me for that position. My colleagues on the commission were obviously a gathering of political clubhouse hacks from every borough—amiable, inter-racial, retired social workers, lawyers and judges, earnest and basically clueless.

Many cases that came to the commission's attention involved parolees who were also drug addicts, which, of course, eliminated any chance for parole. These cases were accompanied with a medical opinion including the addiction diagnosis. We discharged our responsibilities with carefully pompous self-importance, ignoring the obvious conclusion that the job could have been handled by a computer or possibly a trained chimpanzee. Never mind. The positions had been created by the legislature and were perpetuated to serve the political structure in which it existed.

I pointed this out to Steve, but he claimed that changing the system would be too much of a hassle, and to let it pass. I did.

I wonder today if a crusading mayor has discovered the parole commission and saved some money by eliminating it, or at least removed the really obvious cases from its jurisdiction.

During the year or so following my appointment as secretary of the department, the Brooklyn Society for the Prevention of Cruelty to Children (SPCC) invited me to serve on its board of directors. I had already joined the boards of the Brooklyn Institute of Arts and Sciences (which included the Academy of Music, the Brooklyn Museum and the Botanical Garden) and the Association for Mental Health, and I wanted an excuse to avoid any more such affiliations, but Steve urged me to take this one. Later on, I realized why he wanted me to have this experience. The SPCC in Brooklyn, modeled after the hundred-year old SPCA, founded in Boston to care for abused and neglected horses, was a social agency to which our Juvenile Aid Bureau occasionally referred some of its cases. It was a venerable social agency, its conservative, upper-class white staff and board members struggling to understand and deal with the vast gap between their experience and lower-class black dysfunctional conditions.

One case really stands out in my memory. A young black child, about thirteen, had complained to her teacher in school that she was being held against her will by the older man who ran the household where she and her mother lived. The man was a charismatic minister who ran several boarding houses for unmarried women and their fatherless children, all members of his "parish." The child alleged that the whole operation was really a private bordello for the pastor, and when a daughter of one of his mistresses reached puberty, she was expected to join the harem.

Outrageous as this seemed to the SPCC, the caseworkers had to admit that everyone concerned seemed prosperous, happy, thriving in school, well-nourished, and they adamantly opposed to having the arrangement terminated by court order.

During the year or so I served on that board, we took no action on this case beyond anxious talking and waiting.

The heavy, clumsy tools available to the SPCC (a court order followed by referral to the overloaded foster care system) seemed to be a worse alternative than leaving the child right where she was.

I never learned what happened to the girl. The following year I became a deputy commissioner and had to quit the SPCC.

I may have given the impression that Steve Kennedy was my closest associate in the department, and I did see a lot of him, but I saw and worked more closely with five of my immediate colleagues, with whom I became very close.

Walter Arm, deputy for community relations, was wise beyond belief in the ways of both policemen and reporters. He saved me hundreds of times from being too garrulous in dealing with the press. James Kennedy, first deputy, was a tough Irish professional, an incorruptible, strong Catholic, but far from being a patsy for the cardinal. He led his squad in frequent raids on known drug dealer's lairs, and took me along on one raid to show me what police work was really like. The squad broke down a door in West Harlem, a furious dog lunged out, and the squad shot the dog dead in its tracks. No evidence was found.

Aloysius J. Melia was the department counsel, running the legal bureau. Before I appeared, he was the only attorney on Steve's staff. He handled legislation, served as liaison with the corporation counsel (the city's lawyer) regarding all suits against the department, department trials and citizen complaint board cases. He was a superb, canny, tactical advisor.

Jim MacElroy told me all I needed to know about the complicated license division, and Bob Mangum, a marvelous, street-smart black man, a former lieutenant, became one of my best friends. Years later, as a Court of Claims judge, he officiated at my marriage to Phyllis, my second wife.

One of the happiest discoveries I made during my years in the department was the respect I felt for virtually every black person I had anything to do with, Bob Mangum especially. It affected me deeply, and was confirmed over and over during the following years of pubic service I experienced,

There was plenty of discrimination against Blacks that I saw among white members of the department: for an outrageous example, PAL had never allowed any of its Harlem or Bedford-Stuyvesant bands to march in the St. Patrick's Day parade until I became in charge.

Jim Foley, the director of PAL, said to me it wouldn't be appropriate; they weren't Irish! I called Cardinal Spellman's office to see if they would have any objection. I spoke to an officious monsignor. He said that the archdiocese had no objection to Blacks marching, but that PAL was discriminating by having all-Black bands.

I pointed out to him that no white kids ever volunteered to play in a Harlem or Bed-Stuy band, and that, in my judgment, only allowing our lily-white Staten Island bands to march in the parade constituted discrimination.

When he continued to be adamant, I closed the conversation by informing him that he should check with the cardinal, because I intended to remove all PAL bands from the parade and put out a press release about our conversation to explain our position.

The following week, my police liaison with PAL informed me that the parade sponsors had invited all PAL bands to march, including the two black ensembles.

Steve Kennedy himself personified the kind of color-blind policy attitude I most admired. Before his day, when a black officer graduated from the police academy, he would routinely be assigned to Harlem or Bed-Stuy, where he might stay for the rest of his career. Prior to 1950, one might live for years in Manhattan's East Side without ever seeing a black patrolman. Steve changed this policy when he was chief inspector, and stuck with it when he became commissioner. He was the first commissioner to appoint a black deputy, Bob Mangum, who was previously precinct desk lieutenant.

9

Angel's Pal

On December 1, 1958, a hideous fire destroyed an uninspected parochial school in Chicago named Our Lady of the Angels. For two long days, this tragedy crowded local news off the pages of all the New York papers. Ninety-two children and three nuns were killed. I had just been appointed acting deputy commissioner for the New York City Police Department's Division for Youth, and I realized that the same thing might happen to Police Athletic League ("PAL") facilities under my supervision. I had also just been to The Bronx, where one of our PAL centers was in a condemned fire station with an open stairwell, clearly a violation of the fire code.

I asked Jim Foley, the amiable Irish retired police inspector who was the "director" of PAL and who reported to me, if any of our centers had ever been inspected for fire violations. He looked absolutely blank. PAL was incorporated as a not-for-profit corporation, and I asked him if it had a liability policy. Another blank look. Finally I asked him if Fox Lair, the summer camp PAL owned in the Adirondacks, had ever been inspected. Again, he didn't know.

I was appalled. This was staggering mismanagement, and I was in charge. I decided that every piece of property in which kids were served by PAL must be inspected, and every violation must be corrected. Further, until this process was complete, we had to close everything down. Thousands

Steve Kennedy was my boss and inspiration for my years in the NYCD. He was utterly incorruptible, played no politics, and saw the department through racial disturbances and the most difficult era of youth crime waves the City had ever seen. He changed me from a timid Wall Street lawyer into a confident public administrator in four intense years. Photographer unknown.

of kids and their families would be impacted, and they'd be furious. The Police Department's most vaunted anti-delinquency effort closed for months? Impossible!

That, by the way, was Jim Foley's reaction. I think he felt that if I did this, the public reaction would result in my being removed from my office, and he probably hoped this would happen.

Several factors helped me in my decision: Commissioner Steve Kennedy, my boss, knew this was the only sound approach to such a situation. Moreover, the chairman of the board of PAL was a tough Irish banker who felt the same way.

Finally, I had the uncommon good luck that the city's first great newspaper strike began that very day! I issued a press release that afternoon announcing we were temporarily closing all our facilities, and not a single newspaper was there to hassle me. TV and radio reported the news, but we did need to get the word out. I arranged to have each center director call all of his clients, and that was that. Then I asked Police Commissioner Kennedy to call his counterpart, Fire Commissioner Cavanaugh, to arrange a crash inspection program of all PAL centers. All of the inspections were performed before the newspaper strike was settled. The fund-raising machinery of PAL shifted into high gear and private contractors around the city did most of the work required to comply with the fire inspectors' findings. Everything was finished in less than two months.

Above all, the people of New York City understood that we had done the right thing. I was, and still am, proud that I knew what to do, and that I stuck by my guns and did it. I never found out for sure, but I believe that my decisive action in this episode ultimately led to my being elevated to become deputy commissioner, without the "acting" in the title.

10

Was I Officer Krupke?

In September 1957, *West Side Story* opened on Broadway. Based on Romeo and Juliet, the music was composed by Leonard Bernstein, with choreography by Jerome Robbins. It was a huge hit, and ran for 732 performances. The show portrayed the era of gang wars on the streets of New York, and it exactly coincided with the two years when I was charged with fighting gang wars with the New York City police. One of the characters in the show was a bumbling patrolman named Officer Krupke, and my friends began to call me by that name.

In the late 1950s, many people still perceived juveniles as small adults, as they had been viewed in the eighteenth century. If a juvenile committed a crime, there were those who felt the child should be punished.

The more modern approach was that treating juveniles as adults was extremely counter-productive, and a variety of more lenient actions should be taken, ranging from a mere warning through counseling and all the way up to psychiatric treatment, before even considering a prison sentence. A related development was the recreation movement, which began in the 1930s. It assumed that delinquency could be headed off in all children by keeping them so busy that they couldn't get into trouble.

FBI Training Conference. Alexander Aldrich demonstrating youth weapons confiscated by NY cops. 1957 NYPD staff photo.

A combination of these approaches characterized the youth justice field when I got involved in 1957, and the NYPD had three programs that reflected a strong commitment to each approach.

The Youth Squad, a highly trained, hard-hitting group of young male cops, was created for the purpose of squelching the fighting street gangs. The squad was created to meet force with force. About sixteen hundred men were assigned to these units at any one time. They were evaluated frequently, and as vacancies occurred in the detective squads, the best men were elevated to the detective division with a substantial pay raise. The result was predictable: young men who showed promise craved assignment to the youth squads; if they did well and "kept their noses clean"—stayed honest—they were rewarded. It was a continuing inspiration to me to be responsible for such a group. Moreover, since my part of the job was to command the youth squads, I came to regard myself, indeed, as the closest approximation to Officer Krupke I was ever likely to become.

The Juvenile Aid Bureau had a totally different philosophy, a lenient one: any arresting officer had the option to refer the offender to the JAB for investigation. The JAB officers, usually older and more mature than youth squad men, were trained in social work and were often but not always policewomen. They would interview the kid and the parents, examine the kid's record, look at the nature of the offense, take information from school records, and finally make a quasi-judicial decision about what should be done. Eighty percent of the JAB's cases were closed by issuing a warning. Ten percent were deemed serious enough to result in referral to family court on a charge of juvenile delinquency. The remaining ten percent were referred directly to a social agency for attention. These cases were often runaway girls or abused children, who needed protection for a variety of reasons.

The Police Athletic League (PAL) was the department's version of the recreation approach to youth problems. Created in the 1930s, it supplied city kids with five drum and bugle corps, and more than four hundred sports teams, mostly baseball in the spring and basketball in the winter. There were twenty-five PAL centers staffed with social workers and coaches, art programs, a summer camp in the Adirondacks, and a formidable city-wide boxing program.

As deputy commissioner for Youth Programs for the NYPD, I was responsible for running all three of these complex divisions.

A troubling sidebar to the mainstream philosophy was the one that saw delinquents as "victims of society," who should be somehow protected from vindictive policemen and judges by sympathetic social workers. Another problem was the frequency we found parents who were in total denial about the behavior of their own children when they were caught in an act of criminal behavior. "My child is a good boy!" followed often by "The cop made a mistake!" Another was the difficulty faced by police was attempting to locate parents at night when their kids were on the street committing crimes; some of those parents were out doing the same thing!

Still another huge complication arose from the number and size of the six huge bureaucracies involved in the "Youth Problem." They were:

a) The police, whose programs I have described.

b) The schools, which fought to keep the police off their property.

c) Churches and synagogues, many of which provided "youth clubs," a small minority of which tried to attract gang members by giving them sanctuary.

d) Social agencies, almost all of which were extremely helpful in providing referral facilities the police used extensively

e) The courts, especially the Family Court which had jurisdiction over children under 16, and the criminal courts at 100 Centre Street, which had two parts: one for seventeen- and eighteen-year-olds, and the adult criminal courts which handled older teenagers and adults. Even in the family court, which had about fifty judges citywide, there was a very wide discrepancy among the judges when it came to the frequency of findings of delinquency (for under-sixteen perpetrators), or guilty (for those over sixteen). One could often predict the result from the character of the judge before whom the child was taken. There was "Turn 'em Loose Bruce," who hardly ever made a finding of delinquency. Some of the older, tougher judges had an 80 percent conviction rate.

f) The press. Interested in bad news, this bureaucracy tended to be fair to the police, but was far too quick in reporting a "crime wave" if it could be made to appear so.

Financial Problems at PAL

A few weeks before my arrival as deputy commissioner, Jim Foley, PAL's director, called a special meeting of its board to announce a fiscal problem. PAL was facing imminent bankruptcy. Unaware of the irony of his actions, he offered to send his PAL-financed car to pick up the board members to bring them to the meeting.

By the time I was appointed, some members of the board had contributed enough money to buy a little time, but I was urged to start an emergency program that would finally fix matters in that troubled agency. I immediately began to move on three fronts.

I asked the Rockefeller Brothers Fund to back a management audit, and they promised support. The moment he learned about this, Foley submitted his resignation, which I gratefully accepted.

I undertook a personal visit to every program. This took a lot of time, but most of the centers were convenient and busy and filled with kids from the neighborhoods, with arts programs, counseling programs, marching drum and bugle corps, and the best boxing programs in the city. I was very impressed with the quality, size and variety of the programs, and that everything was operated by enthusiastic, seasoned, civilian professionals.

My last visit was to Fox Lair, the PAL camp in the Adirondacks. In the early fall of 1957, I flew on Mohawk Airlines to Glens Falls. I was met by Earl Allen, the camp's maintenance man, who drove me in his station wagon northwest into the Town of Johnsburg for what seemed to be one hundred miles, on roads that got worse with every mile. Our destination was the Siamese Ponds Wilderness.

A twelve hundred acre former "Great Camp" once owned by perfume magnate Richard Hudnut, Fox Lair had been the favorite hideout of Rudolph Valentino, the former lover of Hudnut's daughter, during the 1920s.

When Hudnut died, he left the camp to PAL, one of his favorite charities. The big mansion had burned down, but there were many outbuildings that were suitable for housing campers, as well as one very nice cottage named Commissioner's Cottage, where Jim Foley stayed in the summer.

Earl was verbose, telling me many details about the many police inspector friends of Jim who used to come, often bringing their own children, to enjoy the salubrious air, the lake swimming, and the hiking. He also filled me with gossip about Valentino and the Hudnuts. I departed that night with the unreal feeling that Fox Lair had become Jim's "perk," and an expensive one at that. I had a very hard time squaring the existence of Fox Lair with PAL's stated purpose.

Indeed, I was able to persuade the board of PAL to accept an offer from the state Department of Conservation to purchase the entire property. Foley could not use his influence to stop this wise decision. In one dramatic action, we added substantially to PAL's endowment, eliminated a major annual expense, and added substantially to the forest preserve of the state.

Overhauling PAL's Fundraising

In the early years of PAL, according to Steve Kennedy, PAL had the reputation of sending precinct patrolmen out with a summons book in one hand and a PAL subscription book in the other. It was a not-so-gentle shakedown; if the tradesperson failed to support PAL, what followed was an inspection of the premises followed by a summons for whatever violations the cop might find.

In the 1930s and 1940s, more sophisticated fundraising techniques were developed, based on programs developed by Catholic Charities and other sectarian groups. PAL developed a list of regular contributors, held an annual drive, and a commerce and industry drive, too, which was always heavily supported by banks and the construction trades, as well as their unions, which were heavily Irish and Catholic. There was also a drive within the police department and other city agencies. What was missing was a major society component, and I decided to create this.

I asked my first wife, Elizabeth, to suggest a chairlady for the purpose. She made an inspired suggestion, which I jumped at.

Peggy Bedford Bancroft was the lady's name. She had been a debutante when I was in my twenties. She was almost unbelievably beautiful, slim, with curly blonde hair, a wonderful figure, and enormous energy, just too good to be true! Soon after her coming-out year, she had married Tommy Bancroft, a rich young New York banker. They looked like the ideal couple.

Peggy had a simple ambition: to become the number one hostess and social leader in New York City. She persuaded Tommy to buy an apartment at 71 East Seventy-First Street, in the same building occupied by John D. Rockefeller, Jr. Peggy then embarked upon a fiercely expensive round of party-giving. With the help of a young Italian named Lanfranco Rasponi, a professional public relations man, she flooded the society pages with press releases, and in a short time her beautiful face was everywhere.

I called her at her apartment, left a message with the maid, and that afternoon she returned the call in her patented, breathless fashion. I said, "I'm planning to throw a major charity ball next winter for PAL, the first one ever, and we want it to create such a huge splash that it will become an annual event."

"OMYGOD!" She shrieked, "I'D ADORE TO HELP!"

"Can you meet me at Youth Division Headquarters next Thursday at eleven?"

"Of course, darling. Can I bring Lanfranco?"

"Bring anyone you want, Peggy."

The following Thursday she arrived at 34½ East Twelfth Street in a Lancia, her chauffeured town car. Her escort was a nice-smelling, polished, pomaded young man with an obsequious air, a smooth Italian accent, and a clipboard. No sign or mention of Tommy Bancroft.

She had already selected the venue for the ball, the old Astor Hotel on Times Square, which was scheduled for demolition the following year. She had also picked the date, late in October. I approved both choices, and told her that she had to serve as the ball's chairperson. She agreed, of course, and said she would handle the invitations and supply PAL with her entire guest list, as well as full public relations services from Lanfranco.

We all agreed that special entertainment might be supplied by PAL, and I suggested the Wynn Center Drum and Bugle Corps, an all-black group of one hundred teenagers from the Bedford-Stuyvesant neighborhood in Brooklyn. For the first time, Lanfranco intervened, and suggested that he and Peggy audit their act first. Knowing how superb these kids were, I readily agreed.

I set up the audition with some care. I went in person to the Wynn Center to tell the musicians to make their best effort that night. Then I picked up Peggy and Lanfranco at her apartment in my official car, a large black Buick with a huge, burly, Italian detective driver, Sal Mancuso. We took them across the Manhattan Bridge and started to show them Brooklyn for the first time.

Approaching Wynn Center, I saw a small crowd of black parents around the main door. Peggy responded like the star she was, shaking hands and smiling and saying hello in her "Locust Valley lockjaw." Lanfranco looked scared to death. Sal Mancuso regarded him as if he were some sort of exotic bug.

The Wynn Center director was in his element. He greeted us at the door, ushered us up to the balcony, and signaled to strike up the band. Muffled drums beat a slow rhythm: boom bap ba boom, bap ba boom, boom, boom; boom bap ba boom bap ba boom, boom, boom. Then with a blast, ninety-six brass instruments lifted the roof off the building, and one hundred big black boys and young men came marching across the floor, accompanied by majorettes, playing an arresting African march, with a leavening of Latin sound! It was sensational, deafening, and perfect for the planned occasion.

Both Lanfranco and Peggy were stunned and Lanfranco turned to me and put both thumbs in the air. For the next hour the band played other numbers, and we planned the Astor event, deciding to have the Wynn Center Drum and Bugle Corps play just one short piece: the first, stunning one we heard, with no majorettes. The band would then march off to the same beat, leaving the audience yelling for more. On the night of the party itself, that is what really happened.

Peggy delivered everything she promised. Fifteen hundred invitations went out, and one thousand tickets were sold at $150 apiece. Peggy's favorite florist decorated every table free of charge. The Mayor and Mrs. Wagner came; so did Commissioner Kennedy and Hortense, his wife.

We tried to do everything right. Peggy came backstage with me after the corps had performed to let them know how fantastic they had been. Between the two of us (and Lanfranco), we had put PAL on the society map, and assured its financial future for quite a while.

Morning Conferences with the "PC"

From my first days as secretary of the department in 1956, I was treated as a full member of the police commissioner's "cabinet," although I never fully felt so until after I was sworn in as a full deputy commissioner. By 1958 I had proved myself to myself, and I began to render reports to the whole group with confidence at our Monday morning conferences. Early in my new role, the aging deputy commissioner of licenses retired. His office was across town on Vesey Street, and he was responsible for taxi licenses and cabaret licenses, as well as licensing of cabaret employees. Historically, all of these functions had been handled by the city license commissioner, but so corruptly that a "reform movement" transferred them to the more honest Police Department!

To my astonishment, when the old guy left, Kennedy appointed me "acting" deputy for licenses, while he sought a full-time replacement.

During the three weeks of that assignment, I got a complaint from a *New York Post* reporter (a friend of Peter Braestrup, my brother-in-law), that the Village Gate, a very well known bistro in Greenwich Village, had large numbers of unlicensed workers and many other violations. I knew that one of the daily tasks of the youth squads was to visit and inspect licensed premises for violations, especially for serving minors. I immediately sent over a large group of youth squad members to do a full audit of the Village Gate, and they found that every license was in order, all employees were licensed, and that the management was scrupulous in checking IDs at the door. Even the soap dispensers in the ladies room were filled and had adequate supplies. I reported back to Peter that he could go there safely.

Attending the commissioner's staff meetings was an irreplaceable experience and training for me in my later role as a state commissioner. I learned how to run a meeting and, on some occasions, what to avoid. For instance, Steve had a very short temper and would occasionally lash out angrily at one of his staff in front of everyone else. I never did this; it isn't necessary. It is a form of bullying and it was the only fault I could find in the man.

He also held daily press meetings, at which he was masterful. Once, the *Post* reporter said he had information that police sometimes substituted for each other, and asked if the PC opposed this. Without blinking, he replied, "Reporters do the same thing, don't they?"

The chastened reporter looked guilty and mumbled "Good answer, commissioner."

The only time I saw Walter Arm, the communications deputy, mess up a press conference occurred on a day when a *Daily News* reporter inquired why so many policemen couldn't prevent every crime. "Unless we have advance warning, in a free society, the police are helpless to prevent a random act of violence." The next morning, the *News* ran a banner headline on the front page: "POLICE HELPLESS IN CRIME WAVE, ARM ADMITS!" I learned that day not only not to smile, but also never to use a word that would look bad in a headline.

Studying at NYU

When I started in the department in 1956, I knew little about how the City of New York was organized or how the various departments and agencies functioned and interacted. Happily, New York University offered a superb masters degree program in public administration and social services, and I found that they would give me credit for the M.S. in taxation courses I earned in 1952 while at Milbank, Tweed. I started taking courses in the spring of 1954 at the NYU Night School at Washington Square, and kept it up until I received my M.P.A. in the summer of 1960. That spring, I wrote my master's thesis, the topic of which was "A Centralized, Coordinated Department of Parks, Recreation and Historic Preservation for New York City," which outlined the reasons for and the methodology involved in combining all those functions, then spread amongst eight different city agencies, into one powerful department. It would have merged parks with school playgrounds, PAL, recreation in hospitals and prisons, and so on, with major savings in supplies and personnel. I won the NYU prize for the best M.P.A. thesis that year.

Two years later, the mayor hired a consultant to examine recreation in the city. The final report looked suspiciously like my thesis, and I learned that the next time I write something, I should copyright it.

Commencement took place at the Bronx Campus of NYU that June, next to the Hall of Fame for Great Americans. I proudly stood in my Harvard Law robes, next to my four children and Elizabeth. It was a very proud day.

Teaching at City College

I had enjoyed a close relationship with Deputy Chief Inspector Bob Gallati, the commander of the police academy and the holder of two Ph.D. degrees, one in education, and the other in public administration. He was one of my strongest supporters when I was secretary of the department, and always got my support in strengthening the academy. Before I switched to the Youth Division, Bob asked me to support him in creating a joint program between the Baruch School of City University and the Police Department, to offer courses at City University in police science. To my excitement, I was soon named co-chair of that department along with Professor Katz of the Baruch School as my co-chair. I learned a lot about higher education in that assignment, which stood me well in several of my later lives. The program we developed later matured into the John Jay College of Criminal Justice, and I have always been proud of the role I took in getting it started.

The next step was to actually start teaching there. One of my final jobs as secretary was to represent the commissioner in planning for the annual conference of the International Conference of Chiefs of Police (IACP), which was scheduled to occur the following year in San Juan, Puerto Rico. I was sent there for a whole week, staying alone in the Hotel La Concha, a beachfront high-rise on the San Juan waterfront. I attended a series of agenda meetings that could have been held in a New York City hotel, except for the fact that most of the delegates spent much of their time either swimming or playing in the hotel's casino. Feeling and acting like a complete nerd, I took the opportunity to find out as much as I could about delinquency prevention and treatment in Puerto Rico, which I figured would be useful if my temporary assignment as acting commissioner for youth became permanent. I visited station houses all over the island, interviewed judges, and studied Puerto Rican juvenile law. I took copious notes, absorbed them on the plane home and, on my return, I figured I could teach a course in the subject at Baruch. I offered to do so, Katz approved it, and the following semester I began teaching at Baruch on Monday and Wednesday nights. This schedule allowed me to continue my courses at NYU, which were on Tuesday and Thursday. I maintained this schedule for the following two years.

During that first semester of teaching, I had a class consisting entirely of students from the Juvenile Aid Bureau, most of whom were extremely bright policewomen. One of them in particular stands out in my memory: Felicia Spritzer.

One evening, she stayed late after class and asked me for my advice. "Commissioner," she asked, "why can't I take the sergeant's test?"

"I can't imagine, Felicia," I replied. "Why can't you?"

"They say I cannot, because I'm a woman!"

"That's crazy," I said. Then I remembered my lawsuit against the city comptroller back in 1954, which I won.

"Felicia, here's what you must do," I proposed, "visit the ACLU, ask them to appoint you an attorney, pro bono, and sue the city, the mayor, the Civil Service Commission and the police commissioner for a court order compelling them to allow you and any other qualified woman to take the test." She looked appalled, and replied "I couldn't do that, commissioner!"

"It will never change if you don't," I said. "If you don't, Felicia, who will? You owe it to yourself and all your qualified colleagues to take the lead." That was the end of our conversation.

About seven years later, I read a small article in the *New York Times*. The headline read "Policewoman Spritzer appointed Department's first female sergeant."

A few years later, another headline announced her retirement as a lieutenant. I was very proud of her.

Teaching the course in Puerto Rican juvenile delinquency to that class was a supremely satisfying experience for me, and it led me ultimately to another rewarding career as a teacher.

11

From Minnow in the City to Big Fish in Albany

The summer of 1959 was extremely busy, both for me and for the youth squad I commanded, the youth gang fighters of the New York City Police Department. I still maintained a full evening course load at New York University, and I was still teaching at City University.

At the same time, I had coordinated an effort to smooth communications among the Street Club workers in the city Youth Board. The latter were mostly young male social workers who had, until then, looked at the police as enemies from whom their clients, the gang members, should be protected. On several occasions we discovered that some of these social workers were serving as "drops" for their gangs, allowing them to stash their arms with the Street Club workers when the cops came around. They were trying to ingratiate themselves with their clients, but it was quite illegal and, to put it mildly, unproductive.

Before the summer began, Mayor Robert F. Wagner, Jr. called a meeting of all the commanders of both agencies and their top staffs at police headquarters. In that meeting, the Street Club workers agreed to inform their own supervisors whenever a "rumble" was scheduled. The supervisor, in turn, would call the youth squad office immediately, and a team of cars would be dispatched to the area. That summer, my office received sixty such calls, with the result that, in some cases, there were more cops in the affected neighborhoods than there were gang members. By September there was a significant fall-off in street gang activity.

Even so, there were some isolated, headline-grabbing events. It was a very hot summer, and there were still a lot of disaffected youths in the streets of New York. In August, on a hot Saturday, a couple of them, nicknamed "Cape Man" and "Umbrella Man," shot and killed a boy in a vacant lot in Chelsea on the Lower West Side. One week later, a similar event occurred in Harlem. Another week went by, and a young woman, Theresa Gee, was shot from a car while she sat on the steps of Morris High School in The Bronx. The media went nuts, making it look like the city was completely out of control. Mayor Wagner, appointed a committee to look into the matter and demanded an immediate report with recommendations. I was an active member of the committee. One committee member recommended that no child be allowed to enter a school with a "pointed instrument." I asked, in mock innocence, whether that might include a pen or a pencil, to point out what a foolish suggestion that was, but nevertheless, over my objections, that language was ultimately included in the committee's recommendations. Happily, when implementing legislation was proposed, that foolish idea did not survive.

While the mayor's committee was laboring, Governor Rockefeller appointed his own committee under the distinguished chairmanship of Eli Whitney Debevoise of the New York Bar. They did a much better job than our committee, recommending a new division in the executive department under the governor, to be named the Division for Youth. Its mission was to prevent delinquency by creating machinery to intervene in a kid's life when he or she was first caught in an illegal act. Thus, their focus was to be on first offenders.

Less than a month later, Commissioner Steve Kennedy asked me to represent him at the annual Brooklyn Sunday

School Picnic in Prospect Park. There were about half a million people there, mostly black, and every major political figure in the state. (It was an election year.) I spotted Governor Rockefeller on the dais, and went over to say hello. He grabbed me and said he was thinking about a new job for me, and asked me to discuss it with Bill Ronan, his all-powerful secretary. I promised him I would.

I learned that he wanted me to head up the new Division for Youth. He wanted a lawyer with public administration and law enforcement experience, and my name kept coming up.

I had been awarded my master's degree from NYU in June, and I decided it was time to leave the Police Department. I foresaw that the media would always credit my appointment to nepotism, but I intended to try to blunt that by showing fair-minded people that I could do the job well.

Adding to my police experience and my education, I decided to tour major European countries to research their youth problems, to see if they had any answers that hadn't been tried in the U.S. I took Elizabeth and all four children with me, sailing on the *Volendam* immediately after the NYU commencement, with a shiny new "Honorary Deputy Police Commissioner" shield in my pocket, presented by the commissioner, and an International Association of Chiefs of Police button in my lapel. Both were to serve me well.

We landed in Rotterdam after a lovely, gentle Atlantic crossing, loaded the children—aged two, four, six and eight—into a rented Volkswagen bus, and started driving. Almost immediately we began to notice angry faces, rude gestures and aggressive drivers cutting us off. I quickly figured out that the cause was the "D" (for Deutschland) on the back end of the car. The citizens of Rotterdam loathed Germans, and liked to show it! I quickly stopped at a bookstore, bought a small American flag, and taped it over the "D." People started to smile and wave.

We drove into the countryside and stopped in a tiny town named Streefkirk, at a small hotel surrounded by windmills. Our travel agent had advised us that every hotel had a very large attic room with lots of beds, which they rented to youth groups and large families. We stayed in that type of accommodation all the way across Europe.

Our first official visit was to the Danish city of Odense, the birthplace of Hans Christian Andersen, and home to a world-famous farm for delinquents. Sponsored by the national government, operated and presided over by the most loving couple I had ever met, the farm buildings were built around an enormous square courtyard. There were dormitories on one side, cowbarns on two, and housing for the couple and other staff on the fourth.

I asked them what the recidivism rate was for their charges, and they blithely said that nobody ever got into trouble again after they left there. Basically, it was a benign work camp in a socialist society, which kept track of everyone all the time, regardless of what offenses had been committed.

I was impressed with the people, if not the system.

After a side trip to Norway, I spent a day in Stockholm, where a young and very knowledgeable woman in the social services office gave me a complete rundown on the entire system, which was highly complex, with many and varied resources. At one point, I asked her at what phase they actually stopped taking care of a child who had gotten into trouble. She looked at me in disbelief, and said, "Never, really. We follow them for the rest of their lives!"

From Sweden, Elizabeth and I went to Helsinki, and to Stalingrad for a brief visit to the Winter Palace and Czar Szelo. We ended up with a week in Moscow, where authorities apparently knew I was related to the Rockefellers, for they assigned a secret policeman as our Intourist guide. When he wasn't with us, we were followed clumsily by plainclothesmen wherever we went. I told our guide I had worked in delinquency prevention and treatment and wanted to see how they handled the problem, and he huffily proclaimed that the communist world had no such problem, so there was no need for a program.

Elizabeth returned to Norway to be with the children, and I went alone to Vienna, to examine the fascinating programs there. Every possible group had a separate program:

the government, the Catholics, the Lutherans, the police, at least one hospital, a couple of labor unions, and so on. Some programs were residential; some were not. I visited them all, but saw very little I wanted to replicate in America. As I expected, the emphasis was heavily Freudian. I tried in vain to get accurate statistics. I got the impression that success in a program was measured by how the staff felt their charges were doing.

Later, back in London, I met a lot of police officials, including Miss Bather, the crisply efficient head of all the policewomen in Scotland Yard. She arranged for me to go on patrol with two of her best patrolwomen: a burly, strong woman in her late thirties who could have overwhelmed the Green Bay Packers' forward line, and a lovely, petite brunette in her early twenties.

We spent several hours patrolling Soho, where nothing much was occurring until we passed the mouth of a cul-de-sac alleyway. A huge fistfight was raging in the alley, with about twenty men involved. The small policewoman bellowed, "Wot dyer think yer doin?!" Everyone froze.

"Why nothin' ladies," was the reply, "just havin' a bit of a roughhouse!" The fighters dispersed. I asked the younger woman if they had Judo training, and she cheerily replied, "No, but everyone thinks so!"

On another evening I patrolled again, this time with a tall man with a police dog. Never had Soho been so quiet! He told me he had never had to use the dog in a direct confrontation with anyone except in a training session. I realized that this idea might work in an all-white area like London was in those days, but that it might backfire terribly elsewhere, as it did in Birmingham, Alabama a few years later, and in Rochester in 1964.

The following day I took a train out to the Borstal Training Center, a correctional program for adolescent boys. It had recently been immortalized by the great Irish poet Brendan Behan, who had been an inmate there. It was located in a large, grim, nineteenth century prison, about ten miles south of London. I arrived there in a freezing rainstorm, but I was pretty impressed by the quality and dedication of a staff that seemed, cheerfully, to make the best of a truly depressing place.

The next visit was to a new social experiment, an "approved school." Clearly named by a bureaucrat who wanted to hide its true purpose, the place was an experiment in applying military discipline to the delinquency problem. Located in a field near London and staffed by retired top-sergeants from the British Army, all of whom resembled sharks, the program seemed designed to imitate army basic training, but instead of learning to shoot, the trainees spent their days building chain link fences, all by hand. It was grim, repetitive, hand-cranking work, and the end product of a day's work was about half a mile of material that would be used to enclose the next batch of delinquents. It was grim, and I heard later the project was discontinued fairly soon after I left.

The final visit was to a genteel center not far from Wimbledon, intended for uncontrollable teenaged girls. I went there for lunch, and was interviewed for more than an hour by the young inmates. They all wanted to know if I knew Elvis Presley, and when I told a little white lie and said I had met him, they all squealed with excitement. The girls were all dressed conservatively, except for several who had exaggerated pointed toes on their shoes. I gather it was the latest rage in the teenage delinquent set. They all asked if I liked the fad and, picking my words with great care, I replied that I did not, because I felt that a female body needed no exaggeration, anywhere, to approach perfection. That answer seemed to satisfy them.

I returned to the United States at the end of the summer, buoyed by the feeling that nobody had a better answer to the delinquency problem in America than I did. I was sworn in right after Labor Day, and headed for Albany to begin my work.

I took office on October 1, 1960. The legislature had passed the new law creating the youth division that spring, Chapter 881 of the Laws of 1960. It amended a 1945 law creating the old youth commission, with its small staff and budget of $6 million a year, channeling state aid to local governments for recreational programs. Chapter 881 added new ideas about delinquency prevention, including residential programs and a much larger budget. It was then my job to make it all happen.

I started by meeting the members of the commission who, except the chairman, were kept on as advisors to the new director. They were most useful, especially Millie Aulisi of Gloversville, a friend of Malcolm Wilson, the lieutenant governor. I also promised the small existing staff in Albany and the field representatives in various communities around the state that I expected them to stay on. For the most part, they also proved extremely helpful. I realized I would need my own management team, and persuaded two essential people I knew to come with me. The first was Bill Hambrecht, who held a Ph.D. in public administration and had been my right hand at the NYPD, especially in achieving the personnel records program. I named him my deputy for administration. The other was Milton Luger, head of the education program at the Riker's Island prisons, who had helped me write part of my NYU thesis. I named him my deputy for youth center programs. They were both inspired choices, and they began working immediately.

We hit the ground running. I charged the group with breaking ground for our first youth center on March 14, 1961, my thirty-third birthday. We almost made it. I also asked each of the field reps to find one or more available pieces of property in his or her area as a site for a possible center. Luger suggested creating a number of forestry camps in rural areas, and a series of START centers (Short Term Adolescent Residential Treatment) in urban areas, patterned after the Highfields program in New Jersey, which was then the latest model for treating first offenders with intensive group counseling methods.

I then embarked on statewide trips to see how the old system of state aid worked, and also to size up existing staff members. I developed an instant liking for Lou Pierro, the engaging field rep in the City of Hudson, and an equally negative judgment about Fanny Lawson, the field rep across the river in Ulster County. For the following three years I had many opportunities to discover how right my early judgments had been. Sebring, the field rep in Syracuse, was an able conniver, who wore both of us out in a lightning-quick three-day tour of the entire central New York region, from Binghamton to Lake Ontario, from Canandaigua to Utica, all in his state car. I am firmly convinced he wanted me to regret coming out there in the first place—and I did. The Niagara Frontier rep was the commission's expert on local Indian tribes, and thus irreplaceable. The Long Island area was entirely and ably handled by Ersa Poston. There were eleven field areas in all, which made operating the entire division fairly easy. The reps were a mixed lot, from highly able and eager to help, to fairly unmotivated civil service bureaucrats: it was a lot like the police department, and I felt right at home.

There were two regional administrators who had supervisory roles over the reps: Ersa Poston, stationed in New York City, an immensely able woman who was married to Ted Poston, the widely known black columnist for the *New York Post* and a critic of the governor. My first instinct was to let her go right away, but for many years after, I was delighted that I restrained myself. She was a gigantic help, not only to me but also to Nelson. The other administrator was a tiny, easy-going Jewish guy from Kingston, stationed in Albany. He talked a fine line of cooperation, but when it became time to do some real work, he let us down. I resolved to get the most out of all these men and women, and for two years I thought everything was going pretty well.

There were a couple of other holdovers in Albany: our budget officer, who wasn't very helpful, but who was made irrelevant by the skills of Bill Hambrecht; an amiable but lazy PR officer named Jack Maranville who left of his own accord; and an able black lawyer, Allston Crawford, who served as our counsel and was also the chairman of the Albany NAACP, a connection that turned out to be useful to me later. For a while, I asked him to stay on as our assistant counsel, and I brought in Jack Blum from Milbank, Tweed to serve for a year to help me get started. He was my best friend at the time, and he was a mighty source of strength. He and Crawford made a wonderful legal team. We also inherited an impossible research director who, as far as I could tell, never did any research before or after I arrived. I gave her a number of assignments, but she never delivered, and her only qualification seemed to be that she had a Ph.D. She insisted on being addressed as "doctor," and one day refused to attend a meeting I had scheduled. I told her I was transferring her to the New York City office, where the real need for effective research was located, and she quit in a huff. Had she not, I might have transferred her to Siberia.

This, of course, provided me with a vacancy to fill. I did a nationwide search, and finally interviewed a man I thought was perfect. He was from the California Corrections Department. He came east for the interview, and I met him when he got off the plane at JFK. We instantly hit it off, and I hired him, assuming, because he already had a state job elsewhere, he had passed the appropriate security clearances that everyone in New York had to pass at that time. That later turned out to be a real mistake.

He was one of the best researchers in my whole experience in government. He insisted upon pure research of programs, measuring success by random selection of subjects, and the use of control groups. He refused to use professional opinions about program success, which is how most social science research was done in those days. He wanted to see results: Did the program graduates go back to school, get a job, keep out of trouble, and do better at those indicia than the controls? If not, the program was a failure. Our own pros were scared to death of him.

Three years later, when I was asked to join the governor's staff, Nelson asked me to recommend someone to succeed me from my division. Without hesitating, I recommended my research director. To my horror, when the state police ran a routine "BCI check" on him, they found out that both he and his wife were card-carrying members of the Communist Party, both in California and in New York! To foist him on Nelson

Rockefeller's cabinet in 1965 would have been a complete disaster, and I was almost duped into doing it. I brought him into the office and confronted him with this information. He turned ashen, and asked me what I intended to do. I told him I would accept his immediate resignation and that I expected him to leave the state. He did so.

When I took office in the fall of 1960 I was thirty-two years old with a law degree, an M.P.A., a state car, a superb staff, the full support of a marvelous governor, four beautiful children, a supportive wife, and excellent health. There were many days I thought I had died and gone to heaven.

I was entitled to a chauffeur, and the local Republican Committee recommended a man from Chatham to drive me. Marty was very nice, but nearly incompetent as a driver. He was terrified of driving at night, and of any place south of the New York City line. I should not have retained his services, but I was always determined to make the most of the material I had, and I tried to train him on the job. I finally realized that I would have to stick him in the passenger seat in New York City and at night. It was a relief when I moved over to the governor's office and could then choose another driver, a black guy from Hudson who was superb and loyal. His only problem was a wife who occasionally called the cops and had him put in jail.

With Luger and Hambrecht running the new show, and the existing staff continuing the old, my principal job was liaison with the governor's office, especially including the budget director, Dr. T. Norman Hurd; the governor's counsel, Bob McCrate; the governor's secretary, Bill Ronan; and an occasional brush with the appointments secretary, Carl Spad. The latter was always trying to foist some political hack off on the DFY. Happily, I almost always had a better person up my own sleeve; the one exception was when Maranville left, and I knew nobody who would be right for the position. Carl recommended a young guy from Ulster County who managed to offend everyone on staff, and several local leaders as well, with his arrogance and bad judgment. Fortunately, he quit to run for the assembly. Incredibly, he won the election, but got bored after one term so he never lasted to bother us.

I also worked very hard to travel the state continuously, visiting local leaders, the press, Rotary Clubs, and doing my homework in staff meetings and keeping everyone on target in both the main office and in the all-important New York City branch. I was using all my abilities and energies, and I was on the crest of the wave.

On April 1, 1961, we opened our first START Program in Middletown, Orange County, Fanny Lawson's area. Luger recommended appointing Wally Nottage, a capable black director from Long Island for that program. A trained, authoritative MSW, he was an ideal choice. Incredibly, Fanny Lawson arrived in my office a few days later to protest assigning a black man to her area. I heard her out, and pointed out that I expected her to be loyal, to explain to her friends that most of the kids in the new program were either Black or Hispanic, and to waste no time in getting to know him and appreciate how perfect he would be. To her credit, she followed my instructions.

The center was located on the grounds of the Middletown State Hospital, in a structure that had been a pigsty when the institution had been the State Homeopathic Hospital in the nineteenth century. It was completely renovated by the state Office of General Services, with huge assistance from the budget director. We had missed our target date by two weeks, but the governor was pleased by our record achievement. Simultaneously, we were building our first forestry camp in Rensselaerville, a remote area in southwestern Albany County. On one occasion I went there to inspect the construction and the temperature was minus forty degrees. I felt sorry for the city kids who would soon be assigned there.

The following three years were filled with similar activities, punctuated by opening ceremonies, which were often attended by the governor. We opened three other forestry camps, and about twenty START centers.

My approach to youth corrections was similar to what I had learned in the NYPD:

a) Recreation, as in PAL. Encourage the average, active kid to engage in sports, the arts, and other positive activities, especially in the summer months when they are out of school.

The former youth commission, whose program still existed and which I now implemented through the field reps, paid half the cost of operating local recreation programs in every county in the state.

b) Social intervention, somewhat like the JAB. This approach was hinted at in the Debevoise Task Force report. Our response was to use a very exciting precedent begun in Highfields, New Jersey by that state's correction agency. We took twenty kids at a time, subjected them for about twelve weeks to intensive, daily group counseling in which the kids themselves analyzed each other with a trained social worker's supervision, and then sent them home. Then we would follow their progress to see if they stayed out of trouble, went back to school, sought employment, and exhibited other evidence of appropriate behavior. Sure, we picked the kids whom we thought would succeed, but it certainly seemed they did, for the most part.

c) Forestry camps, more like the conventional law enforcement approach of the youth squads. In fact it echoed the approach of the corrections department, placing young men in remote forested areas and subjecting them to hard labor in the woods, clearing fire trails, thinning, pruning and other tough tasks. For many inner-city late teenagers, this was a scary and unwelcome treatment that we hoped would make them want to change their ways.

d) Research, something we never did in the NYPD. I always believed that coping with delinquency was an incredibly uncertain science, subject to political influence and every sort of shopping around for a new, less expensive fix for a human problem. We were expected to have the answer, but what was it? Punishment? Psychoanalysis? Social work? Education? Faith-based institutions? Vocational training? I wanted to become the Dr. Spock for delinquency prevention and treatment, and to lead the way to the definitive solution. I tried to establish the necessary research machinery to ask the right questions and gather the necessary data to root out a series of coherent answers. Sadly, I didn't have the necessary forty years to do this.

At the same time I was building on my years in the NYPD and, with the help of Ersa Poston, establishing relationships with the black leadership in New York City. By the spring of 1963 I had established a thriving new state agency, showing how to cope with the delinquency issue, and making Nelson Rockefeller look good in an area close to his heart. The press never got over its habit of referring to me as "the governor's cousin," as if it explained my success. Had I screwed it all up, they would have made hay about it, but I never did screw up.

That summer was the time of the Birmingham church bombings, and the birth of the American civil rights movement. Nobody else on Nelson's staff had as familiar or comfortable a record with New York civil rights leadership as I did. He decided to bring me over to the governor's office as his executive assistant, and assigned me to work directly for him as the cabinet coordinator for human rights. Ten other members of the cabinet were required to work with me, including Attorney General Louis Lefkowitz and the chairman of the Civil Rights Commission. I took office on September 1, 1963, and my first assignment was to go to the civil rights March on Washington.

Before leaving DFY, my last job was to recommend my successor. I've described the first fiasco, with my director of research. My next suggestion was to recommend the superb man who had succeeded me at the police department, Lawrence Pierce. It was a perfect fit, and he spent the next few years carrying on what I had done, with distinction. To my knowledge, none of my successors ever wrote the Spock book on delinquency prevention and treatment. Nor did I.

12

Campaign Loss and Harlem Triumph

In the spring of 1966, many of my friends in Columbia County urged me to run for Congress in New York's 28th District, made up of Columbia, Greene, Schoharie, Ulster and Dutchess counties. It was, at the time, a safe Republican district, which was temporarily represented in Congress by a maverick Democrat named Joe Resnick who appeared to be easily beatable.

I was warmly endorsed by Myrtie Marilla Tinklepaugh, chair of the Columbia County Republican Committee. She encouraged me to pursue her counterparts in other counties and towns throughout the district, and to get involved with the preservation of Olana, the awesome estate of the great nineteenth century Hudson River School artist Frederic Church, located on a splendid mountaintop just south of Hudson.

Church's grandnephew had inherited the property and was negotiating with developers to sell the spectacular land, the Moorish castle at the top, and the art collection. We negotiated with him a price of a million dollars, and I helped to form a committee of community leaders along the Hudson River to raise the funds. Within a few months our new organization, Olana Preservation Inc., was able to raise half that figure. My wife, Elizabeth, was enormously helpful

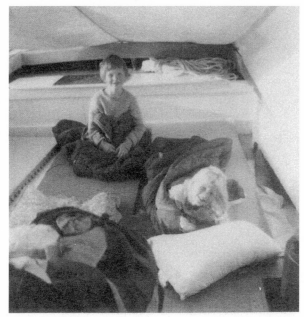

Stern area of *Strider* under canvas cover, Will and Sarah settling down for the night in Green Harbor, Vinalhaven, Me. I took the picture June, 1983.

and involved, and I served as the highly visible and active president of the effort.

I asked Nelson for his support, and he suggested getting the legislature involved to match the private funds and turn the estate into a historic site and state park. With the publication of a spectacular photographic spread in *Life* magazine, which appeared on each legislator's desk the morning of the key vote, the bill passed easily, with the matching funds included, and Olana became state property. I had become well known in the valley, particularly in the congressional district.

I also made it my business to interview various community leaders, including the presidents of a number of local colleges. One of these was the head of the community college in Poughkeepsie, Dutchess County. He gave me the inspiring information that his school was reaching its maximum capacity; within the next two years it would no longer be able to enroll any more students from Columbia or Greene counties.

I went dashing back to Hudson, called a meeting of my closest friends, and we cooked up a plan. We had just preserved Olana, and now we decided to embark on another campaign to get the supervisors of the two counties to create a new community college, and to locate it on the grounds of Olana.

Lou Pierro, who had been my field rep in the Youth Division for that region, and who was now my Columbia County campaign manager, was galvanized into action. He spoke to every member of both county boards individually about the desperate need for immediate action. The Greene County board then called a meeting at Catskill, followed by a similar meeting in Columbia County, at Hudson. I attended both, and got both groups to appoint a joint committee to manage the creation of the college. They also asked me to serve as a member of the founding committee. By the next meetings of both boards, both of them adopted the positive recommendations of the joint committee, and a new community college was launched.

In 1990, at the grand age of 62, I proudly attended the celebration of the twenty-fifth birthday of the Columbia-Greene Community College. I seemed to be the youngest person there.

Today, the college is thriving, with 1,770 students enrolled in a two year academic program offering associates degrees in liberal arts, humanities, business management, criminal justice, computer science and other disciplines; it also boasts a strong athletic program, with intercollegiate men's baseball, men's and women's soccer and women's softball; and a variety of minor intramural sports.

Having saved Olana and having worked to found a community college, I decided to resign as Nelson's executive assistant, give up my state car, and declare my candidacy for Congress. There was one other candidate, Hamilton Fish, Jr. from Dutchess County. Ham was the son of the famous congressman of the same name, whose hatred of Franklin

Roosevelt in the 1930s and '40s had earned him the lasting support of the conservative wing of Republicans throughout the country. The syncopated neologism, Martin, Barton and Fish, had become one of FDR's favorite slogans in his presidential campaign against Willkie in 1940.

I knew Ham well from Harvard, where he had been a year ahead of me at the Porcellian Club. His only experience in public life had been as an assistant to Mayor John V. Lindsay in New York City. I dismissed him as a lightweight. How wrong I was!

Ham had the support of the Republican Committee of Dutchess County, the most populous of the five counties in the district. I had followed Mrs. Tinklepaugh's advice in Greene, Schoharie and Ulster counties, and had courted and gotten to know virtually every town chairman there. At their nominating conventions, four of the five counties endorsed me. By primary day, in June 1966, even though only the Town of Pawling had declared for me, I was fairly confident I had at least an even chance in Dutchess County, and by the Thursday before election day I thought I was a shoo-in.

Then the roof fell. Each candidate was required by law to file a financial statement about the cost of his campaign. It was a series of questions that required simple answers: How much did you spend, did you borrow the money from anyone, who were they, etc.

I worked hard at presenting a truly accurate estimate of every expense I had incurred in the campaign, trying to be completely honest and accurate.

The problem arose when the question came, "Did you borrow any money?" I innocently but correctly said "yes," for I had pledged a substantial amount from my trust fund in the Chase Bank to cover any shortfall. The Fish campaign jumped on on this, with a huge headline that read, "ALDRICH HAS A FRIEND AT CHASE."

It was a staggering, last minute blow from which I had no time to recover. Had I been smarter and less honest, I would have simply ignored the question, since the money was really mine, but the damage had been done and I lost

Dutchess County. I carried the other four counties, but it wasn't enough.

After nearly an entire summer on Spruce Island recovering from my defeat in the congressional race, I went back to Islesboro, where I received an unexpected phone call from Nelson Rockefeller. He asked me to come back to work for him. I thought he was just being kind to me, and I heard myself saying no.

For the first time, he responded quite angrily, and said he really needed me, that he had a job that I was truly suited for, and he wouldn't take no for an answer.

I told him I would be back the following Monday.

When I returned to New York, I was sporting a scraggly beard I had grown on Spruce Island, and a number of the Harlem people I was dealing with thought I had joined "The Movement."

It was 1966, and times were changing.

Nelson had decided to erect a new, impressive state office building at the intersection of Seventh Avenue (now Adam Clayton Powell, Jr. Boulevard) and 125th Street, at one of the most visible points in central Harlem's business district. I had been selected to represent him in the delicate business of communicating with the black leadership there, assuring people that Harlem residents would be selected to work on the construction project. This meant I had daily meetings with Peter Brennan, the head of New York State Building and Construction Trades.

Peter was an extremely warm supporter of Nelson, although both his own union, the Sheet Metal Workers, and the parent Building Trades, had traditionally shown reluctance to allow Blacks to register as trainees in their apprenticeship programs. If you were not Irish, one need not apply. Brennan himself, as Irish as a man can be, saw the foolishness in this position, especially on a building in Central Harlem, and the two of us worked hard to make it all happen. I went to all the church leaders to get black men to apply for the positions, and Peter persuaded the union leaders to open the positions to black men. I did not check to find how well the program operated, but the black leadership appeared to be happy with the results.

I had nothing to do with the selection of the site for the building; that had already been done by the Harlem leadership in a discussion with the governor. The leaders wanted to destroy a large nest of small buildings that housed drug houses on the corner of 125th Street and Seventh Avenue and build a state office building there that would attract a more middle class clientele. Three years after the building had been erected, it became the focus of radical black discontent, but that was two years after I had gone on to other endeavors.

One thing I did succeed in doing was to discover a black architect. Percy Costa Ifill was the founder of the New York City firm of Ifill, Johnson and Hanchard, whom I selected to present the first draft of the plan to the press. The reporters arrived ready to rake us over the coals for hiring a white firm to design the building, and the best thing they could do was to ask me why I had picked this man. I blithely answered, "He is one of the best."

In the judgment of history the Harlem State Office Building has not been a success. Jane Jacobs, the architectural historian, referred to it later as "Rocky's Viet Nam." Radical black leaders denounced it, led sit-in demonstrations in it, and the New York real estate market has passed it by. The junkies and drug dealers that used to inhabit the site had merely moved across the street. The two flagship tenants are the state Office of Housing and Urban Development, and the office of retired President Bill Clinton.

The building is now renamed the Adam Clayton Powell, Jr. State Office Building. It is still one of the very few office towers ever erected in Harlem.

I didn't realize it at the time, but this event established a pattern for the future relationship between Nelson and me. I had become the office "fireman," ready and able to step into a hot spot and provide him with effective service, which was basically designed to make him look good. I was a trained lawyer and public administrator, experienced in race relations, in handling the press, and in working closely with politi-

Harlem Office Building, 1958.

cians at every level. I was also fiercely loyal to him. Thus, this job was followed by my work with the Hudson River Valley Commission, chair of the state Cabinet Committee for Civil Rights, handling the Rochester Riots, and stepping into the Office of Parks and Recreation program when the then commissioner turned sour. The press never really understood what was transpiring; I only figured it out in later years when I had the time to think about it.

13

Rioting 101:
A Man and His Plan

My assignment as the governor's executive assistant started pretty slowly, or so I thought. I had spent a long morning in New York City overseeing the establishment of my new office on the top floor of 22 West 55th Street, which was Nelson Rockefeller's city headquarters. The date was November 22, 1963, a perfectly ordinary day as far as I was concerned. Nelson was in Albany, and at lunchtime I went out to LaGuardia to catch the state plane to join him there. Except for the two pilots, I was alone on the plane. I stretched out in one of the seats about halfway back in the old DC-3, and immediately dozed off after we rose up over Long Island Sound.

The next voice I heard was the Albany Airport ground control telling our pilots that Kennedy had been shot! I was on my feet in an instant, running up the aisle of the plane to confirm what I had heard. Of course, it was all too true.

When I arrived at the terminal I immediately called Nelson. I confirmed that he was in no danger, promised I would be there as fast as I could, and urged him to put all flags at the State Capitol at half-mast immediately. He said he had already done so.

On the way into town from the airport, my mind was churning. I knew that my job would require me to be ready for any future emergency in the state, and that I was as unready to discharge such an assignment as I had been when I first became secretary of the NYPD back in 1958.

When I arrived at the Capitol, I immediately went to Nelson and told him I had to plan ahead as if I knew that the worst would happen, and that I was going to do it whether he gave me permission or not. I posited that, if he were killed or his plane crashed, or if there were ever a race riot in the state, or a prison riot, or a radiation accident, or a huge forest fire, I had to know what response should be planned and executed, what agencies were to respond, what proclamations were required, and what laws might be involved. He immediately agreed, and helped in suggesting some other possible disasters that I might consider, and some agencies like the Attorney General's Office and the Federal Emergency Management Agency which might be involved.

The following Monday I began assembling a staff and a committee comprised of the agencies concerned, and we started work immediately. The State Police, the National Guard, the departments of Conservation, Correction, Law, Transportation, and Budget, the offices of General Services and of Local Government, and the Thruway Authority are the ones I thought of first, and I added others as they were needed. We all felt a great sense of urgency, which was heightened as the extraordinary pageant of the Kennedy funeral was played out before us on television.

The committee and staff labored mightily for six months, finally compiling a complete "disaster book" which identified about twenty major disaster events, with carefully researched responses for each.

For example, one of them was the death of the governor, and it included such details as who would be given the task of notifying the first Mrs. Rockefeller.

Another was the almost prescient possibility entitled "Race riot in an upstate city on a Friday night in the middle of the summer when everyone is on vacation." This one included an 1865 law resulting from draft riots during the Civil War that prohibited the state from ordering state militia to enter a city unless its mayor had announced that he had lost the power to enforce pubic order. This statute reflected the events in 1865 when the New York City mayor, a Democrat, ordered the city police to fight a pitched battle on the steps of City Hall with a squad of State Militia sent in by a Republican governor.

In May I happily informed Nelson that I was ready for anything. I had four copies of the disaster book made up. I kept one in my car, one in my office, one at home, and one in my family's apartment in New York City. Everyone concerned always knew where I could be reached when anything "hit the fan."

During the hot, third week of July, 1964, a series of pretty nasty race riots took place in New York City, mostly limited to the all-black areas of Harlem in Manhattan and Bedford-Stuyvesant in Brooklyn. To my great satisfaction, the city police department's response was massive, professional and completely effective. I went all over the city, frequently accompanied by friends from the Selma March, including Charlie Rangel. We were watching to make sure that the response was appropriate. There was never any need to activate any of my standby plans. By Friday, July 25, the city was quiet, I was exhausted, and I was looking forward to a nice weekend with my family in Maine.

I had a brief meeting with Nelson around noon. "I'm flying to Maine for two days," I said.

"Sam," he said, "I have a funny feeling this is going to be a bad weekend. Stay here in New York."

My rueful response was: "When the governor tells his executive assistant, 'don't go on vacation,' the executive assistant stays at his post."

I cancelled my flight and called my friend David McGovern. "Are you spending this weekend in town?"

"Yeah, dammit," he said. "I have a court appearance Monday morning and have to finish the brief."

"Let's go out and get drunk!" I suggested.

We found a splendid German restaurant on the Upper East Side and followed my prescription.

I reeled back to my parents' apartment on Seventy-seventh Street around 11 P.M., carefully laid out the disaster book by the night table, and fell into a dreamless, rather drunken sleep.

The night was blasted open by the phone ringing next to my head. It was Arthur Cornelius, the scholarly, quiet superintendent of the State Police. It was midnight, and a serious race riot had broken out in Rochester after the city police arrested a disorderly black man. Foolishly, the police had used a canine patrol as part of their response, which enraged the entire neighborhood, and the fat was in the fire! An angry mob of adults and teens had taken over an entire area and were threatening to march on City Hall.

"Who's in charge?" I asked.

"The only person who's making any sense is the city attorney, and here is his number!"

I called the number, the man answered, and in a voice tightened by sheer terror, he demanded State Police, National Guard troops, the 82d Airborne, the United Nations, *now*!

I had opened the disaster book, and in a calm voice I said, "Counsellor, I have six hundred state troopers assembling at this moment at the Henrietta Barracks just south of the city. They will be moving into the affected area at dawn. For you to make this legal, you must take down the following telegram, have it signed by your mayor and sent to Governor Rockefeller." I then dictated to him the language used in the 1865 statute, stating that the mayor had lost the power to control public order and requesting assistance by the state. I also told him that it was statutory language, Chapter 231 of the Laws of New York, amending Mckinney's Consolidated Laws of New York, Military Law, Section 6, and if he or the mayor tinkered with it, no help would arrive. By this point in the conversation, he began calling me "sir."

Then I called Nelson on the line that rang in his bedroom in Pocantico Hills. Nelson answered it on the first ring, and I could hear Happy sleepily protesting, "Who the hell is that?"

"It's Sam," I said, "and we have a big, nasty riot in Rochester."

"Thank God you didn't go to Maine!" he cried.

"That's blasphemy, Governor," I replied. *"You* told me to stay!"

Then I told him what to expect next, that I would be at Pocantico in the morning to get his signature on the proclamation mobilizing both the police and the National Guard (if necessary).

Then I called my New York City secretary, a wonderful, cool, German woman named Greta, and asked her to meet me at Fifty-fifth Street to type the proclamations at nine in the morning.

I called Cornelius again, brought him up to date, and he sent out the order to unleash the troopers. They formed human wedges in the affected streets, slowly advancing and urging people to disperse quietly, which most of them did. Only one person was hurt, a trooper who was hit by a piece of flying glass, scaled at the line by an angry woman. He was the only casualty of the entire operation, as far as I know.

The next morning, Saturday, I met Greta at our office on Fifty-fifth Street. It was eerie; we were the only people in the building. We prepared a series of proclamations, drafts of which were in the disaster book, mobilizing the State Police, predated by a day. Another one for the National Guard was not to be dated until the decision was made. I stuffed them into my NYU briefcase and zoomed up the Saw Mill River Parkway to Pocantico Hills.

I was warmly welcomed by Nelson and Happy, who forgave me for disturbing their sleep. I said that I would never do it again—unless he again spoiled my weekend in Maine.

From Pocantico, I called Art Cornelius to see how things were going, and he reported that all was apparently quiet in Rochester. Nelson had signed both proclamations in case the riots started up again, and authorized me to act immediately to mobilize the National Guard if it was clear that the State Police needed more manpower.

I spent the rest of the morning trying to find the commandant of the National Guard. His office was closed. I called his home; his wife said he was at the Winding Brook

Club in Chatham. I called the pro shop, and they sent a golf cart out to the sixth hole to get him. He called back, wondering what all the fuss was about. None of this was covered in the disaster book. I told him the chances were very good that we would need to alert him that evening, and he assured me that all was ready. He gave me an emergency number to call, which I added to the book, and then went back to the apartment on Seventy-seventh Street to crash for a few hours. I knew I would be called again soon.

Sure enough, in the early evening my phone rang again. This time Cornelius sounded gloomy and embarrassed. "The rioters have changed tactics," he said. "They've left their own neighborhoods and have begun looting stores downtown. I don't have enough men to cover the whole city."

"Are you getting any help from the Rochester police?" I asked.

He laughed. "They are all on duty, giving out parking tickets in white neighborhoods."

"The Guard will start to arrive within an hour," I told him. "These will be the units from Rochester and Buffalo. They will be directed to drive through the black neighborhoods as noisily as possible, and bivouac in the park nearby. Sixteen hundred are on their way. They are being dispatched from all over the state, in eight-wheeled personnel carriers, and when they arrive they will have their canvas sides rolled up so spectators can see the troops inside, with their weapons. I expect the unit from Montauk will roll in about dawn." I knew that *he* knew that the rifles the troops carried were not loaded. Nor were any of these troops trained in riot control. The last thing we wanted to happen was to have some trigger-happy white kid from Syosset, Long Island, shoot a black woman from Rochester with a state-issued rifle.

As the night wore on the riot slowly subsided, and by morning a tent city had arisen in the park next to the black neighborhood, filled with armed, uniformed white men, happily feeding themselves a hot breakfast. Their rifles were peacefully stacked near their tents. Nobody knew what the orders were for the remainder of the day. A few State Police continued to patrol the black neighborhoods. The city police continued its vigorous enforcement of the traffic laws. The churches of Rochester were full of worshippers, praying for peace.

I like to think those prayers made the difference, but I also think that the presence of a reasonably adequate show of force, coupled with really professional troopers minus the hated local cops, persuaded the local Blacks to cool things off. For whatever reasons, the Rochester Riot ended Sunday night.

Of course, my job had just begun. My worst nightmare would be to pull out six hundred troopers and sixteen hundred guardsmen, only to have the riots start up again.

All day Sunday I furiously worked the phones, trying to find out who the leaders of the riot were, and how to influence them to call things off. I discovered that the only identifiable person that any of my contacts had ever heard of was a charismatic black minister with the improbable name of Franklin Delano Roosevelt Florence, who led a church in the black area of Rochester. He was a disciple of the radical community organizer Saul Alinsky, who for years had fought with Eastman Kodak, not very successfully, for better relations in the city. I spent three straight days trying to corner Reverend Florence, who liked to be called "Minister Florence," either on the phone or in person, but with absolutely no success. When I went up there on Tuesday, I actually went to his church, but he had disappeared.

On the following Tuesday, Nelson called an early-morning staff meeting at Fifty-fifth Street. I gave a full report, and urged him to go to Rochester in person to thank the guardsmen and the troopers for their response. That elicited a storm of protest from other members of the staff, the press secretary, political advisors, and Bill Ronan (his most trusted advisor, known to most of us as "Dr. No!") They all said he would be accused of playing politics, "showboating" and other evil intentions, and was risking more criticism than the trip was worth. After they all had their say, I quietly spoke up: "Nelson, you ordered twenty-two hundred citizens of the state to risk their lives for public safety. You owe it to them to fly up there and thank them personally where they are."

"Sam is right," said Nelson. "The plane is at LaGuardia. Let's go now, but don't tell the mayor until we land at the Rochester airport." He did not want the mayor to take this event over, and he was right. The mayor was quite huffy to him when Nelson called, grumping that he had already been called from the airport, and already knew; Nelson told him it was not an official visit to him, that he was there only to thank the men for their service.

State cars appeared, and the party rolled into the city, arriving at the bivouac in the park in time for lunch. A large canteen had been set up, and the men were beginning to line up to get their trays of food. Nelson was in his element. He shook sixteen hundred hands and thanked each soldier personally. The press photographers were climbing all over the event.

Then he went down to the Henrietta Barracks where the state troopers were stationed, and repeated the exercise. Meanwhile, I borrowed a car and tried one more time to find Minister Florence. I went to his church, but it was shuttered tight. I left a note on the door, but I never heard from him in reply.

On the way back to New York on the plane, we discussed plans about getting the troops out. I told him I was in no rush, but we would start our withdrawal immediately, one truck at a time, with priority going to those who had come the furthest. Thus the first truck out was scheduled to leave on Thursday with eight men from Montauk. Obviously, the rate of departures increased as the summer wore on. The end of September and the cold wind across Lake Ontario saw a complete closing of the bivouac, and no new rioting. The state troopers were also withdrawn with the same sort of relaxed, professional approach, with no fanfare, press releases, or "mission accomplished" rubbish.

Nelson Rockefeller came out of this event smelling like a rose. That was my principal mission in all this. The riots were over, nobody had been hurt (except the one trooper, who recovered completely), I had demonstrated my ability as a planner who could adapt his plans to the demands of the moment, and for the first time in my life, I was impressed with myself. What a feeling!

I have never been certain why those riots never resumed. My guess is that Rochester's white community, led by Kodak and other employers, began a more effective effort to bring more Blacks into the work force. Another thought is that the local police realized their community relations program needed a complete overhaul, and they got rid of the canine patrol. I also suspect that some members of the black community sincerely realized that trashing their own neighborhood, and then the city's shopping district, was both self-defeating and stupid.

I still can't help thinking that the moderate response by the state was a decisive factor.

Whatever happened to the disaster book? Was it ever used again?

Two years after the events described here, in 1966, I resigned my position as executive assistant to the governor, and with some ceremony, turned over all four copies of the book to Alton Marshall, my successor.

"Al," I told him, "this is the most important file I can bequeath to you. Always keep it with you. Spend staff time every year keeping it up to date. The next time you need it—and you will—you won't have time to do it all again!"

Al soberly promised to do this.

And then he forgot all about it.

On September 9, 1971, the huge, maximum security state prison in Attica, Wyoming County, was seized by prisoners. The corrections department had foolishly concentrated every incorrigible, violent male criminal in the state prison population at this one facility, and it had created an explosive situation. The inmates attacked an inadequate force of guards, took over the prison yard, tied up some of the guards there and threatened to torture them and kill them if their demands weren't met.

By then, I was president of Long Island University's Brooklyn Center, trying to cope with a rebellious faculty, and rather glad I didn't have to worry about Attica or pull out the disaster book.

But then I suddenly got a call from Al Marshall. It was the tenth of September, and he was sheepishly asking if I had kept a copy of the disaster book! He wanted the chapter on handling a prison riot.

My first reaction was one of just barely controlled rage.

"Al," I said in a trembling voice, "You must have forgotten our conversation. I warned you that you would need those volumes, never to let them out of your sight, and always to update them. What happened?"

"They've disappeared," he said.

"You are on your own, Al," I said. "There were no other copies."

What happened next has been amply reported. There was a five-day standoff at the prison, while the commissioner of correction and Al tried unsuccessfully to negotiate with a group of completely incorrigible black convicts who controlled the prison yard containing about thirty captive prison guards who were threatened with death or castration or other forms of torture. The confrontation continued in front of an audience of several hundred state troopers on the walls, itching to shoot into the crowd.

Finally, on September 13, in a perfectly ghastly finale, a fleet of state police helicopters roared over the walls, sprayed tear gas all over the crowd, and then the police, lined up on the walls, fired more than three thousand rounds of shotgun, rifle and pistol shots into the yard. Everyone on the walls was white. Almost all the prisoners below were black, except the pathetic crowd of corrections officers whom they held hostage.

The final casualty total was: twenty-nine prisoners and ten corrections officers, all shot by state police.

Under the cover of the assault, other police and officers burst into the prison and restored control. And then a terrible revenge was wreaked on the prisoners who were left alive. Many later alleged being made to run gauntlets of club-wielding officers, and to kneel on broken glass. A congressional investigation was held on the matter, and a class action lawsuit by prisoners led to a settlement of $8 million against the state.

Years later, when Nelson was appointed vice president, a reporter asked him if he had any regrets about his years as governor. "Yes," he said, "I would have handled Attica differently."

It is easy, in retrospect, for me to say how I might have tried to perform a better job. To begin with, I would have been far more patient. Negotiations with angry people should be allowed to mature over time. Nelson himself should have been a party to the talks. Guns and tear gas from the walls of a prison were as inappropriate as loaded rifles would have been in Rochester. The families of the prisoners should have been brought in to reason with them.

There should have been a plan. But, even with a plan, it's possible that nothing would have worked under the circumstances. The most radical of the prisoners were quite ready to sacrifice themselves to dramatize their unhappy lot. The troopers and guards on the wall were completely unwilling to retreat from their positions without shooting at the prisoners who had been taunting them. The fact that they shot three thousand rounds was a measure of their fury and frustration.

A plan, of sorts, was later developed. From that day on, the Corrections Department ended the dumb practice of concentrating all the worst inmates into one prison. When guards noticed a buildup of incorrigibles in one facility, they moved some of them around before they could effectively amass the same kind of riotous presence that existed at Attica. So far, that seems to have worked.

Or, maybe, the state has just been lucky. Might Attica happen again? My answer is "*yes,*" and I hope there is someone in state government who is thinking about that possibility.

14

The Hudson River Valley Commission and Storm King

The Consolidated Edison Company of New York (Con Ed) was one of the several giant utilities fifty years ago that provided the state with its enormous supply of electricity, and had the tremendous responsibility to plan for power needs at least a decade before they became evident to the general public. It previously had taken at least that long to plan a big generating plant.

That was before the arrival of the environmental movement.

By 1962, downstate New York was oversupplied with power capacity. The Indian Point Atomic Plant in Westchester County was capable of supplying substantially more power to the area than it needed in the early part of the day.

That year, Con Ed announced its plans to construct a pumped-storage plant behind Storm King Mountain on the Hudson River, near Newburgh, at the north entrance to the scenic Hudson Highlands. Water from the river would be pumped up about a thousand feet to a man-made lake behind the mountain, in the very early morning hours when power was plentiful. During the day and until about 10 P.M., when the power demands peaked, the water would flow back down and generate that extra needed power. The steady power

The Record

WEDNESDAY, JULY 3, 1968

RIVER STUDY—Dale Bath, graduate student, prepares to lower special net into Hudson River to collect samples of water and its marine life as part of a co-operative pro-

gram between the Hudson River Valley Commission and New York University, Alexander Aldrich, at helm, is executive director of Hudson River Valley Commission.

—Staff Photos by Edwin Conroy

Pure Waters Impact Studied

News article in Rockland County paper showing author at *Strider*'s helm with an NYU team to test water quality off Indian Point atomic plant in Westchester, 1968.

needs were supplied by atomic energy from Indian Point, and when more was needed, a similar facility out on Long Island Sound was to be built.

Strangely, nobody anticipated the foaming reaction of environmentalists to this proposal. A road that cut across its face since the nineteenth century already disfigured Storm King Mountain. The intake vents for the water were to be tucked neatly under the Erie Railroad tracks that ran along its base. The area behind it where the lake was to go was federal land used by West Point classes. The economic growth of New York City and Long Island depended on the development of inexpensive power for the foreseeable future, and Con Ed assumed its proposal was both logical and unobjectionable.

A one-syllable, four-letter word was one of the keys to the level of rhetoric that ensued: "Shad!"

The fish, whose delicious roe has for centuries been one of the great delicacies supplied by the Hudson, was found to spawn in the shallows north of Storm King. I do not know who discovered this fact, but it soon took on biblical proportions. Another key was the existence of a strong lobby for gas-generated turbine engine companies, wanting to sustain customers' desire to use their product to supply peak demand for power. Still another key was the perception that New York State Governor Nelson Rockefeller, who never saw a vast public project he didn't like, was clearly in favor of it, and the Democrat leadership in Westchester County and elsewhere in the state was eager to clip his wings. The final key was Robert Moses, whose years of arrogant building of highways, housing projects, power plants, dams, bridges and every other kind of public resource—including nearly the whole state park system—had accumulated enough resentment among those dislocated by his programs that he deserved the title Founder of the Environmental Movement. By 1965 a very effective organization was formed for the purpose of stopping the Storm King project: Scenic Hudson Preservation Conference. Its executive director was Rod Vandivert, a former lobbyist for the gas turbine generating industry, but its board of trustees consisted of many very influential civic and environmental leaders both in New York City and the Hudson Valley. They sued in federal court that year to oppose the Federal Power Commission's approval of the Con Ed plan. In the time-honored tradition of political leadership, Nelson appointed a blue ribbon committee to address the problem and make recommendations. Chaired by his trusted and enormously able brother, Laurance, and directed by Conrad Wirth, former head of the National Park Service, it was created by executive order and named the Temporary Hudson River Valley Commission. It was charged only with making recommendations, and was given a year to produce them.

They recommended making the commission permanent. The legislature agreed in its 1966 session, and that autumn Nelson asked me to head it up. I seemed to have become the

Laurance S. Rockefeller was my boss twice: He was chair of the Hudson River Valley Commission from 1966 to 1968, and chair of the State Council of Parks from 1971 to 1979. He was Nelson's younger brother, a world-famous conservationist, and chair of the New York Zoological Society.

office "fireman," ready at all times to step into the hottest spot. Laurance stepped down as chairman and was replaced by an Albany banker named Frank Wells McCabe, and I started in December of 1966. The statute charged the commission with concern for the "scenic, historic, recreational and natural resources" of the area *and* its "commercial, industrial and economic development." I always took the second part of the charge to be just as important as the first, although most of my environmental friends found it irrelevant and annoying.

Before starting to work for the Hudson River Valley Commission (HRVC), I had to talk to McCabe, a man I knew slightly as the president of an Albany bank. He invited me to have lunch with him at an extremely expensive French restaurant that he owned, Auberge des Fougères. I was met at the door by Yves, the obsequious *maitre d'*, and ushered to a round table for twelve where Frank was already installed on his throne—he had lunch there every day, often alone, sometimes with a large group.

Frank greeted me warmly, announced that he had already ordered my lunch, a delicious veal creation, and then sat back and asked how he could help me. I informed him that Nelson had indicated he wanted me to become the executive director for the commission, and I didn't wish to serve unless he, the chairman, approved the appointment. His answer almost floored me: "I would have no objection at all! I would resign, of course, and you would have a completely free hand."

I studied McCabe's face for a second or two. He clearly wasn't joking. His pink, genial face showed no particular animosity, but there was no trace of uncertainty either. I decided to act as if I hadn't heard him properly, and I forged ahead to explain to him how grateful I was for the opportunity to serve him, why I was well qualified for the job, the many experiences I had enjoyed at Olana Preservation, my contacts in the valley during my campaign, my experience at the State Division for Youth and within the executive chamber.

Then, as soon as I dared, I dashed back to my office in the Capitol, and ran breathlessly in to Nelson to tell him what happened. Nelson merely laughed, and said I had handled McCabe perfectly, and told me not to worry about it.

"He is too vain to resign!" he said to me. "I'll handle it."

"I don't want to work for a man like that," I said.

"You won't be," he replied.

I found out later that Nelson had called him the same afternoon and thanked him for being so cordial to me and for agreeing to stay on as chairman. McCabe then said to him that he had serious doubts about my ability and experience, but he would see to it that I didn't make any foolish mistakes.

I later experienced a number of events that confirmed my first impressions about our new chairman. For one thing, during the first days of our activities he was consistently late to commission meetings, sometimes up to three quarters of an hour. This infuriated the other members, and after the first time it happened we simply chose a chairman pro tem who presided until he arrived. He was deeply irritated by this but he began to get the message, and after a few months he began to arrive before the meetings started.

One of the best members of the commission was William H. Whyte, the distinguished author of *The Last Landscape* and a widely known regional planner. During their very first meeting, McCabe said to him, "I read your book."

"What did you think of it?" asked Whyte. "I found it jejune!" sniffed McCabe. The word "jejune," according to *Encarta World English Dictionary*, means:

1. Uninteresting and intellectually undemanding;
2. Lacking maturity or sophistication;
3. Lacking or not providing proper nourishment; and
4. Not very fertile.

Needless to say, Whyte knew the sense of the word and was deeply offended. I have to admit that during three years of working with McCabe, I always treated him as if he was a real chairman, while always going to Nelson or Laurance for advice on policy matters. McCabe treated me in a very condescending fashion, but on administrative and policy matters he left me very much alone, and avoided ever giving me any advice. Without discussing it at all, we had somehow worked out a *modus operandi* that allowed the commission to operate effectively. At the end of the three years, when we were saying goodbye to each other, he admitted that I had surprised him by doing such a good job in spite of his early doubts. Then, in a conversation with Nelson repeated to me later, McCabe took credit for bringing me to top form and saving me from making too many mistakes.

In our last meeting McCabe confided in me that his one ambition was to become the chairman of the Taconic State Park Commission, and asked me to suggest that to the governor. At our next meeting, before leaving to become president of LIU, I made the suggestion.

Nelson laughed at me. "He's impossible! He would always be in our hair down in Westchester. I was hoping you would be available for that position."

I accepted like a shot, and I never heard how McCabe found out, or what his reaction was.

Planning and zoning are local functions in New York State, and jealously guarded. Any state agency which is given power to plan, delay, or change a proposed land use has to be very careful, even when the legislature has given it that power.

The HRVC had to tread very carefully to avoid the appearance of arrogance or of riding rough-shod over local officials. We were created by the legislature, and we could be—and ultimately were—destroyed by it.

We inherited a very good professional staff from the temporary commission that had been assembled by Laurance with Connie Wirth; I had an assistant, an ecologist, an attorney, an industrial geographer, an urban planner, an architect, a landscape architect, a historian, an economist, and a public relations man. I was the lawyer and the expert in public administration. Our tools included the power to hold public hearings on any project proposed for our statutory area: on or in the river, the lands on both sides within a mile of the river, or up to two miles if one could see that far. After each public hearing, we had the power to recommend changes to the design of the project, or to approve or disapprove it entirely.

The recommendation was required to be published within thirty days of the public hearing, and if the original sponsor of the proposal chose, the project could then proceed. In short, we could embarrass and delay a developer for thirty days. However, I decided this would eventually backfire on us if that was all we ever did. I recognized right away that many developers who wanted to do things right might be grateful for the opportunity to use our staff in their planning, and also to get local government officials to do the same thing.

I first began meeting with these officials in a systematic way, and the following spring, when the ice went out and the weather warmed up, I began taking them out on the river in my boat, *Strider*. Still later, at the beginning of my second year in this office, I started a series of "Next Decade" conferences on a county level, asking business leaders, local officials, environmental leaders and newspaper editors from each county in the valley to give us their recommendations about our statutory area.

That, more or less, summarizes our planning efforts. How successful they were was hard to gauge. Because the federal courts were already reviewing the Storm King Mountain project—and that process would take a decade)—we never came close to reviewing that proposal.

Nevertheless, we were soon faced with a number of other important proposals, including one for a Niagara Mohawk atomic power plant and cooling towers in the Town of Easton, Washington County, across the Hudson from the Saratoga National Battlefield; a poorly designed solid waste dump in Yonkers; and Georgia Pacific's request to locate an enormous gypsum wallboard plant on the river at Little Stony Point, just a mile north of West Point. (Our staff found an appropriate alternate location for that imposing project in an industrial zone in Haverstraw.)

The Niagara Mohawk atomic power plant in the Town of Easton was vigorously opposed by local citizens, historians, pure water interests, and by the *New York Times*. This gross invasion of the battlefield's viewshed also attracted the attention of the National Advisory Council for Historic Preserva- . tion (which I would later join and chair). Both commissions disapproved the proposal, and to our mutual astonishment the Atomic Energy Commission withdrew the funding. The plant was never built.

On my first day on the job, I received a letter from Georgia Pacific, asking permission to locate a large gypsum wallboard plant on the Hudson at Little Stony Point, a mile or so north of West Point, in the most scenic heart of the Highlands. I mobilized the staff to search for a more appropriate site. Raw gypsum is a powdery white mineral, mined in Nova Scotia and imported in sea-going vessels. It is made into sheetrock, used everywhere for modern wall construction. We needed to find a place near deep water, a railroad, and with access to major highways near New York City. We found a perfect spot in Haverstraw, Rockland County, which had no scenic impact and was in an industrial area. There the plant is presently located. This was a successful example of what a state commission could do to preserve aesthetic resources from industrial ruin, but nobody ever gave us credit for our efforts.

About ten years after we saved Little Stony Point, Pete Seeger, the great environmentalist and folk singer, arrived in my office at the State Park Commission, with his lovely wife, Toshi, and asked for my help in getting permission to moor the Hudson River sloop *Clearwater* at Little Stony Point. It gave me great satisfaction to do this, and it was accomplished with my help.

Throughout my years as commission director, I was always alert to the need to woo local governments along the river, to encourage local officials to use our resources. I didn't want them viewing us as a threat to their land-use powers. I started holding conferences in every county seat focusing on that part of the Hudson River in that county. Each conference included all local officials who had anything to do with land use planning: town attorneys, zoning boards, building inspectors, town historians, supervisors, business leaders and state legislators. I admit that I was still interested in a second congressional campaign in 1968, and so I concentrated these meetings in the 28th Congressional District. Ham Fish had lost his election campaign there in 1966, and the incumbent soon died in the embrace of a Las Vegas prostitute. leaving an enticing vacancy appeared on the area horizon. Fate intervened again, though, in the form of a spectacular New York City real estate entrepreneur, William L. Zeckendorf, Sr., the man who had assembled the land where the United Nations now stands and sold it to the Rockefellers, who was now recovering from an $80 million bankruptcy. Bill was then in his sixties, intent on rebuilding his real estate empire, and had decided to risk all on the development of the Newburgh waterfront, on the Hudson River just north of Storm King Mountain. It was an exciting idea, given that Newburgh was sixty miles from New York City, outside the jurisdiction of the corrupt International Longshoremen's Association that controlled the docks there. Bill envisioned a big, deep-water port with excellent rail connections on the West Shore Division, and a direct shuttle to the small commercial airport several miles inland. Truck traffic would connect directly to the New York State Thruway, which was even closer. He and I began to plan the program with a growing sense of excitement.

One afternoon, while this was going on, he offered me a lift to New York in his limo. This was the era when only a privileged few had a car phone. We were comfortably ensconced in his enormous back seat when suddenly a phone rang. He reached behind my head, pulled out a white phone receiver, and said three words. "Yes," "Absolutely," "Goodbye."

Then he turned back to me and announced, "I just bought the Essex House," which was an enormous luxury hotel on Central Park South.

I often wondered if that event had been staged for my benefit.

He then offered me the presidency of Long Island University in Brooklyn.

15

Board Memberships

When I first moved to Brooklyn Heights with Elizabeth, I found myself besieged with requests to serve on various charitable boards. I was flattered, of course, and felt obliged to accept what I thought was quite an honor. They were the Brooklyn Institute of Arts and Sciences, which included the Botanic Garden, the Academy of Music, the Museum and the Children's Museum; the Brooklyn Association for Mental Health; the Brooklyn SPCC; and the Parks Association of New York City. I was aware that both my parents served such organizations in Manhattan and I imagined it was an important part of being an adult.

I dutifully went to meetings, worked on various projects they sponsored, and very occasionally made a modest contribution to their coffers.

Later, as I became more prominent in city affairs, the memberships became more important and demanding. I joined the boards of the New York Zoological Society (the Bronx Zoo and the Brooklyn Aquarium), Teachers College, Columbia, and the American University in Cairo.

After moving to the Saratoga Springs area, I also joined several boards here: Yaddo, the artists' retreat, and the National Museum of Racing. It was only then that I began to understand what the true purpose of being a charitable

Author, in retirement, opening Hudson Crossing Park, summer 2005; picture by Libby Smith.

trustee is. It is summed up in the three W's: Work, Wisdom and WEALTH!

I had always been exemplary in the first two of the W's, serving on committees, and spending lots of time traveling to Cairo, once going there three times in one year on committee service. I also supplied the zoo with hay from my farm in a drought-stricken year, and accompanied an aquarium team up the Hudson to chase an errant seal.

But that is not enough! Trustees of charitable entities are expected, above all, to supply them with all the endowment they need. It helps enormously if a trustee is either an officer of a foundation, or, better, the possessor of a charitable foundation of his own—or simply is as rich as Croesus!

It helps if you also are skilled in making appeals to government agencies of other foundations, although most charities have staff who are paid to do this.

I spent a lot of time at Teachers College during the Columbia riots, meeting with disaffected students, and had a modest hand in heading off having their students join the radicals across 120th Street. Never mind. When the time came to reinstate me as a trustee, Bill Parsons, the chairman, told me gently that he thought it was time for me to step down.

I seemed to have been wise enough, and I worked more than anyone else on the board, but I concluded I wasn't wealthy enough!

Possibly because of my casual and flippant attitude towards finance, it was not until 1989 when I was first offered a position as a board member in a serious corporate business—indeed, a new national bank!

The Saratoga National Bank and Trust Company (SNB&T) opened its doors on July 1, 1988, taking advantage of a new law allowing more than one bank to have a main office in our city. Prior to that date, the only bank in our town had been the Adirondack Trust Company, a state-chartered bank.

ATC is a great institution with superb leadership, but it suffered from a lack of competition. Glens Falls National Bank, seeing the opportunity, created a holding company, Arrow Financial, and two subsidiaries: Glens Falls National, and Saratoga National. They needed Saratoga Springs civic leaders to serve on their board, and I was one of those chosen.

Had Newman ("Pete") Wait, ATC's chairman and my best friend, still been alive, I would have turned Saratoga National's offer down. He had recently died in a tragic fire at his Lake George retreat. I thought it over, and decided it was a good thing for Saratoga, and probably for ATC, and accepted. Pete's widow took years before she spoke to me again, although Charles, her son and Pete's successor, has told me more than once that having SNB&T as a competitor revitalized ATC.

I joined the board shortly after its doors opened, and they were going through all the usual growing pains a new company must suffer, adopting policy documents and hiring staff, most of which required board approval. The president of the bank had worked in Glens Falls for years, and was able, and accustomed to following directions from his superiors there. He relied on them to supply him with first rate assistants, and also such documents as bylaws for the corporation. At one board meeting, he laid a set of bylaws in front of us, which none of us had ever seen, and asked for a motion for adoption.

I quickly scanned the first page, spotted a typo, and raised my hand. "I refuse to approve bylaws I have not read, and which obviously has an error on its first page!" Consternation! The offending document was withdrawn, corrected, submitted before the next meeting, and then approved by the board.

The president still hadn't learned his lesson, however. Several months later another proposed document came down to us from Glens Falls, concerning policies to be followed by bank employees. Once again it was presented to the board without prior notice, and again it had a typo, this time on page two! Again I refused to consider the document, and insisted on reviewing it thoroughly.

It was filed with bankers' jargon, but I waded through it laboriously and discovered that much of it simply repeated language lifted from the federal law. I redrafted the language entirely, and pasted together a spreadsheet with the proposed policy on the left side, my comments in the middle, and a revised version on the right.

I started with a paragraph that, in effect, said that every employee was expected to know and follow federal banking laws as amended, thus making it unnecessary to change bank policies each time the laws were amended. Then I eliminated everything that repeated the law as then applied. Finally I included the few things that were left over.

The final draft was brief and easily remembered. The president submitted my draft at the next meeting. I happily moved its approval, and it was adopted. I think I earned my director's fee for that effort, and I hope the president realized I was trying to be helpful, and not just embarrass him and his draftsmen from Glens Falls.

Saratoga National was a huge success over the next ten years, contributing significantly to the success of its parent, Arrow Financial. Since directors were not only paid for going to meetings, but also in periodic infusions of Arrow stock, which has grown and prospered mightily over the years since, my service to that board has been most rewarding for me.

16

Nineteen Years with Nelson

Even though I was Nelson Rockefeller's first cousin, I was always in awe of him, aware of his position as governor, deferential to him as my superior, and cognizant that his vast experience and knowledge of public life was immensely superior to my own. My sense of humor sometimes made it difficult not to poke fun at some of the formalities of gubernatorial behavior, like the parties Nelson gave for the press and the legislature at Pocantico Hills, but I never shared those thoughts with him. I worked very closely with Nelson Rockefeller for nearly nineteen years, first while he was governor of New York State, and then again when he was vice president of the United States. I served twice as a member of his cabinet in Albany, first as director of the State Division for Youth, then later as commissioner of Parks and Recreation. In both of those capacities, I was more in contact with his staff than I was with him directly.

I worked more closely with him when I was appointed his executive assistant in 1963, a position I held for three exhausting years. After that I took a vacation from him, first to run for Congress, and later to serve as president of Long Island University in Brooklyn. Even then I served as volunteer chair of the Taconic State Park Commission, whose jurisdiction included all the state parks in Westchester County and

Formal portrait of Nelson Aldrich Rockefeller, taken by governor's staff photographer prior to 1979, handed to me with inscription on my retirement as parks commissioner.

this, of course, was an area of great interest to Nelson, John, David, and Laurance, who lived there.

It is difficult to describe this man adequately without falling into hyperbole. His almost inhuman physical strength and energy dominated every room he entered. These qualities were always coupled with his view of the future, which set him apart from anyone else.

His memory for facts and figures was prodigious; I once heard him debate a persistent reporter who asked him why he had cut the state's budget for social services. Nelson challenged the reporter's figures, quoting from his memory what the budget had been the previous year.

In my dealings with Nelson, we never once shared coffee, or a meal, or an alcoholic drink. On one occasion, at a reception in Pocantico, I actually noticed him sipping a glass of Dubonnet, a form of vermouth then popular among older society ladies who abhorred hard liquor.

We never had lunch together in his office. I am not even certain that he ever ate lunch. Even when he was the luncheon speaker, my guess is that he didn't touch his food. I never saw a picture of him stuffing food into his mouth, although the press photographers were dying to get one.

Even during the Rochester riots, when he joined the troops at their lunch in the park he didn't eat; he simply stood with each man in line and expressed his thanks to each one.

Was he always "on stage?" In many ways, he was. He could be absolutely exhausted after a red-eye flight from California, and then spend a whole night driving around Albany thanking Niagara Mohawk linemen for their efforts in restoring power after a blackout. That act would restore his energy. He got a similar charge from a visit to an art museum, or more obscurely, searching through art catalogues looking for pieces of modern art available to buy.

To my knowledge, these were his only forms of recreation. No golf, no sailing, no tennis, no workouts at the YMCA. Maybe he did some of these things with his children or his brother Laurance, but certainly never with any of his colleagues or with me. He was quite burly, with strong shoulders and a crushing handshake. He certainly was abstemious; he never smoked or snacked or exercised. I once heard his brother David boast that the only exercise David ever got was when he served as a pallbearer for his friends who exercised. Nelson could have said the same thing.

What do I remember about his home life? Not much, I am afraid. His first wife, Tod, was a remote figure to me. She had been a Philadelphia socialite, and my first wife had the distinction of having been born in the same hospital on the same day as Nelson's firstborn son, Rodman, in 1932. That startling statistic gave my then mother-in-law some boasting rights at the time, but hardly brought the two families closer together. I saw Tod a few times during the final years of their marriage, but I was never impressed with her closeness to Nelson, or her sense of humor. She was stiff, remote and strictly formal with me and my first wife whenever we met her.

As far as I know, Nelson never bothered to carry any money with him. On one unforgettable occasion, when he went with Happy to obtain a marriage license at New York's City Hall, the clerk asked for the usual fee ($10?); Nelson had to borrow the cash from Carl Spad, a staff member.

There are many rumors about Nelson's womanizing. The only time I saw real evidence of this was one night at his home in Pocantico Hills, when he was dancing with the lovely Happy Murphy. It was painfully obvious that the two were completely in love, and they didn't care who knew it. It was soon after this that he announced that his marriage to Tod, his first wife, was over, and he sought a divorce and married Happy.

He was deep in a tough race for the American presidency, and in my judgment the divorce cost him heavily. He persevered, remarried, and lost the primary to Arizona Senator Barry Goldwater. But he won Happy, and had two wonderful boys with her: Nelson and Mark.

Let someone else cast the first stone.

My own first marriage was falling apart while all this was going on. I had met and fallen in love with my Phyllis, soon to become my second wife.

Once, and only once, Nelson invited me to spend the night with him at Pocantico Hills. He had asked me to accompany him to a breakfast meeting with the Hirshhorn family in nearby Greenwich. They were an extremely prominent Jewish couple who had collected an enormous pile of superb modern sculpture which was piled up helter-skelter around their house in the suburbs. I timidly asked Louise Boyer, Nelson's all-powerful secretary, if she could suggest to him that he ask me to spend the night with him so I wouldn't have to ask myself.

She did, and he graciously asked me to drive back to Pocantico with him the night before in his huge Cadillac, and stay in the guest room. I accompanied him in the back seat of the limo, along with two huge briefcases stuffed with documents Boyer thrust into his hands before we left. Our State Police driver drove in total silence up the West Side Highway, then the Saw Mill River Parkway, and finally off onto local roads through the impressive gates of Kykuit, the estate of the first John D. Rockefeller, where Nelson now lived with second wife, Happy.

The whole way home, Nelson devoured both of the briefcases, examining every memo in each one, making marginal comments, and then ending with a note to the senders directing them what to do. He apparently performed the same ritual every day. Several of the papers had been from me, and he handed each one back to me, so I would have them twenty-four hours before I normally would have, and could act on them that much sooner.

A scant few of the memos he saved out of the pile, to examine further after dinner.

When we drove up the driveway, I recall seeing a team of men, maybe four or five of them, busily raking the driveway turnaround outside the front door. There were no leaves there, and I could only conclude that they were smoothing the pebbles. I imagine they saved that job to do every day until just before Nelson arrived home.

Happy wasn't home that day; I believe she was in Seal Harbor, Maine. The moment we arrived, Nelson took me on a tour of the art gallery at the back of the house, ending up with an inspection of all the sculptures on the outside, with special emphasis on the relationship of each piece to the view in front and behind it. He was obsessively involved in each one, telling me where he had obtained it, the name and history of the artist, and why he had put it where he had. His affection toward all of these possessions was infectious and most impressive. There was a Rickey and a Calder (whom he affectionately referred to as "George" and "Sandy") and a couple of Louise Bourgeois stabiles that I really admired.

My supper was brought to me by a friendly butler, and I enjoyed it on a tray in the dining room. It was chicken, vegetables, and a glass of water. I don't remember what dessert was, but I do remember that Nelson did not join me for dinner. After supper I simply retreated to the guest room, took a shower and had a good sleep in a very comfortable bed.

I knew that our meeting with the Hirshhorn family was scheduled for 8 A.M., so I rose at seven, packed my bag and explored the grounds for a few minutes, knowing that breakfast was to be later. Before I got too far, there was Nelson again, ready to go.

We were driven over to the Hirshhorn's place in Greenwich. It could not have been a starker contrast with Nelson's spread. It resembled a used car lot, or a junkyard, except there were no school buses or trucks; every square inch of the grounds was cluttered with modern statues, some of them distinguished, others junky and "op-artishly" garish. They were randomly mixed up and piled carelessly next to each other, not unlike some of those bargain antique stores along Route 17 between Rockland and Augusta, Maine. Nelson didn't say anything, but I could tell his aesthetic senses were hurting as we entered the house.

The Hirshorns were thrilled by our visit. Nelson's mission was to persuade them to donate their collection to the State University at Purchase, and he was at his most persuasive. He lathered them with compliments, lauded the works we had just seen on the lawn, and promised to turn the collection into a museum of the arts, to be the centerpiece of the campus of the most important of all the SUNY campuses devoted to the arts. As state parks commissioner, I had been brought along to add my two bits to the mix.

Hirshorn was cagey. It later turned out that he was negotiating with President Johnson to endow a similar museum on the Mall in Washington, and he didn't want to spoil that possibility by making a firm commitment to Nelson. In fact, that is what finally happened. All the rubbish that was stored on the lawn outside the Hirshorn place in Greenwich is now at the Hirshorn Museum of Art in Washington, D.C. Nelson lost the bidding war for that collection, and I know it must have rankled him for years. The only thing Nelson got out of our breakfast was a large helping of bagels and lox. Maybe the fact that he didn't touch any of it queered the deal. I did my part, anyway; I had two helpings—his and mine.

Nelson was always very generous to the members of his cabinet, some more than others. Every Christmas, each cabinet member received a handsome gold-plated desk ornament, engraved with his name and our initials. One year it was a pair of scissors and a letter-opener in a gold case. Another year it was a heavy gold paperweight. Another was an elaborate pen-holder. Yet another was a glass ashtray from Steuben. And a gold-plated blotter holder. I got my share.

Some of his staff flatly told him they could not afford to work at state salaries unless he personally paid them more. The only person I am sure did this was Bill Ronan, Nelson's all-powerful secretary to the governor. There may have been others, and the fact that Nelson had done this came out during senate hearings before he was appointed vice president. It frankly never occurred to me to do ask for a premium, and I am glad I didn't. It was more than enough for me to have served him for nineteen years, for which I drew a generous state salary and many pension and health benefits that I still enjoy.

There was a breath of scandal about Nelson's death. On his retirement from public life, he marketed some of his possessions, especially some great pieces of modern art. Helping him in his effort was a young female staff member, named Megan Marshack. He often went to her apartment near his New York office to discuss plans for marketing these items.

Nelson suffered a heart attack and died during one of these meetings in 1979.

Inevitably, rumors flew. Megan was a scholarly young woman who bravely tried to resuscitate him, called 911, helped while the ambulance crew worked over him, and behaved modestly and with great dignity when the press appeared. Nobody I know well believes she was a *femme fatale* who caused his death. I am personally convinced there was no affair. In my judgment, Megan was no Monica.

I can only testify to some of the things to which I contributed, or watched from very close vantage point as a cabinet member or as his assistant. Nelson was an extraordinarily forward-looking and aggressive player in the environmental arena, and he gets practically no credit for it. Water pollution in New York State had been an issue for more than a century before he became governor. I was present in his cabinet meeting the day he decided to act on the matter.

Every city in New York State used the rivers to dispose of their sewage and storm water runoff. The cost of treating all this had been estimated at around a billion dollars. Not even blinking, Nelson decided at that meeting to seek an environmental quality bond issue, which would raise that billion to underwrite the cost of fixing the problem.

It took about a decade for all of the municipalities to comply with the requirements and to build the necessary treatment plants. The bond issue paid for most of it.

By 1980, the Mohawk River was no longer the largest source of toxic pollution on the Upper Hudson, and when the huge 125th Street sewage plant came online the same year, even New York City was relieved of the title of the most polluting metropolis in the world.

The cleaner things get, the angrier people get about the exceptions. General Electric has finally discovered that cleaning up the PCBs they dumped at Fort Edward many years ago is a good idea. Nelson's example has outlived him.

Thomas E. Dewey was responsible for the New York State Thruway, as important an achievement as De Witt Clinton's building of the Erie Canal. Nelson Rockefeller certainly wanted to be remembered in that same league, for he was, above all else, a planner and a builder. In his twenties, he was in charge of planning and building Rockefeller Center in New York. By the time he was governor, most of the really big projects, like the St. Lawrence Seaway and the Thruway, had been completed. That didn't stop him from planning other huge projects, of course. The first one was a huge bridge across Long Island Sound from Rye in Westchester County to Oyster Bay on Long Island. The other was an even more ambitious bridge from Orient Point on the extreme eastern end of Long Island, crossing Plum Island and Fishers Island, finally coming to rest at Watch Hill, Rhode Island.The first idea met with opposition from every friend Nelson had in Westchester and Nassau counties. The second was effectively vetoed by one of his best friends in Rhode Island, Governor John Chafee.

Frustrated, Nelson had to turn to some less cosmic challenges. The first one was to take on the reconstruction of Route 17, a two-lane road from Harriman in Orange County, across the entire southern tier of New York State, paralleling the Pennsylvania border, serving a long row of rural communities and a small number of old railroad cities, including Binghamton, Elmira, Bath, Olean, Salamanca and Jamestown. Built to federal standards, the road was costly, but Nelson insisted on the necessary money from the legislature In length, it covers nearly 400 miles, as much as from New York City to Buffalo. Nelson also was a leader in the construction of Interstate 81, which went north out of Binghamton near the Pennsylvania border, through Syracuse and Watertown, all the way to Alexandria Bay on the St. Lawrence River and into Canada, a distance greater than from New York City to Albany on the Thruway. At the same time, he pressed ahead to finish the Adirondack Northway, which paralleled 81 near the eastern edge of the state. To stitch the two highways together at their southern ends, he also built Interstate 88, from Binghamton up to the Northway near Albany. Moreover, on Long Island, he pursued the completion of the Long Island Expressway all the way to Riverhead, and assisted in the revival of the Long Island Railroad, by creating the Metropolitan Transportation Authority, which had municipal bonding authority that saved the LIRR from bankruptcy.

When Queen Wilhelmina of the Netherlands came to make a formal call on the governor, Nelson was embarrassed by the slum that divided the Governor's Mansion from the

State Capitol building. True to form, he immediately decided to tear the whole offending neighborhood down and replace it with a splendid new mall and plaza, with a new building for the legislature, a row of office buildings for state agencies, a law center for the appellate courts and the attorney general, topped off with a theater for the performing arts in the shape of an egg and an enormous phallic tower looming over a giant reflecting pool. At the south end was a huge new state education building, with a library, a museum and office space for staff.

The entire concept was to be designed by Nelson's old friend, Wally Harrison, who had helped him build Rockefeller Center. He even arranged to construct an elaborate highway connection to the east, swooping elaborately out of the bowels of the mall to connect with the new Interstate 787, which allowed car traffic easy access to the Thruway and the Northway. The only amenity Wally forgot was a helicopter pad, which I facetiously suggested should be added. Nelson's face lit up, Wally's face fell. They amended the plan to include it, but the Federal Aviation Agency refused to allow it. I always regretted that the Sam Aldrich Pad (SAP) never came to be.

The entire project immediately ran into enormous cost overruns because of the sub-surface material that underlaid the entire neighborhood. After the houses in place were demolished, it was discovered that the soil beneath was a sticky grey mud, the consistency of toothpaste, incapable of supporting the huge heavy structures designed for the mall. Fleets of trucks had to be recruited to remove most of that soil and to replace it with firmer material, and extremely heavy and lengthy pilings down to bedrock were required. An enormous platform was built on top of the acres of concrete that replaced the slum, which contained all of the necessary support services for the structures above, including restaurants, cafeterias, a barber shop and a beauty shop, two vast garages, a conference center, and a stupendous underground concourse that united the whole center for all-weather pedestrian traffic. The walls of that hall were reserved for acres of extraordinary modern art, mostly commissioned by Nelson from the legion of painters and sculptors he admired.

Above the indoor mall, out in the sunshine between the towering structures, stood other art works, notably a Calder and a Rickey, wagging their arms in the snowy wind. Artists and art critics had a field day. Most critics and preservationists panned the entire project, comparing Nelson to Mussolini, and mourning the departure of the "old Albany" which had been so quaint and decadent and so comfortably corrupt.

I admit that I personally felt sad that the old town had been so shockingly changed, but I vividly recall the evening when Phyllis and I took our then five-year-old son Will to a musical event at that plaza, and walked out to the mall from the Egg into an enormous fireworks show.

"Wow!" he cried, "this is great!"

It was spectacular. And it cost two billion dollars. And it earned Nelson a reputation for wasting taxpayer money, which may, in the end, have cost him his shot at the presidency.

Today, when I visit the Nelson A. Rockefeller Empire State Plaza, my regrets about the passing of "Old Albany" have completely faded, partly because there is still quite a lot of it left, but also because the plaza projects an energy and excitement that reminds me so much of Nelson. Characteristically, he broke the mould of the past and replaced it with something vivid and daring.

As if to defy people who were inclined to accuse him of trying to do too much, Nelson also decided to tackle the problem of public housing.

Ed Logue, a dynamic, charismatic man from New Haven, Connecticut, had demonstrated skill in building effective, exciting, publicly financed housing in that sad city. Nelson brought him to Albany and asked what it would take to get him to take on the job of doing the same thing for New York State.

"I would need the power to override local zoning, and also have the power of eminent domain to purchase properties I would need to build the projects," Logue answered. I was told later that he never thought Nelson would agree, or had the power to get the legislature to agree.

Well, Nelson did both, and Logue agreed to head up the newly created Urban Development Corporation (UDC). This creation was quite successful in some areas, notably on

Welfare Island in New York City, where it created a whole new city between Manhattan and Queens, connected with Manhattan by a marvelous aerial passenger conveyance, and to Queens by a small bridge over the eastern channel of the East River. A somewhat less successful project was an ugly brown development in East Harlem which featured a steady cacophony of traffic noise at all hours from the FDR Drive.

Some of Logue's other projects, notably those upstate, got him into such trouble with local officials that the legislature ultimately took away the power of eminent domain, and Ed departed.

There were three other important public policy areas that concerned Nelson deeply: youth, civil rights, and corrections. In the first two areas, I performed a central role; in the third, I was only on the fringe, and I disagreed with Nelson's emphasis. I strongly wish I had been wiser and more effective.

I brought my own knowledge and experience from my police years to the state Division for Youth, and I realized only in retrospect that Nelson paid me a huge compliment by never second-guessing the actions I took during those three exciting years. In chapter 11 I describe what I did, consulting with him on every policy decision, and his enthusiastic support made my job much easier.

Philosophically, Nelson shared my realization that young people, especially black and Hispanic, had a tough time adjusting to responsible adulthood in our society, and when one of them ran afoul of our law enforcement machinery, our traditional correctional treatment might be deeply counterproductive, both to the perpetrator and to the public. Our challenge was to design interventions that were both firm and sensitive, and understood by the youth to be in their best interests.

We both also realized we lived in a political world where "get tough" was perceived by many as the preferred solution, often because it was believed to be the cheapest one, and sometimes because many white people in our society felt this was the best way to treat black and Hispanic kids.

In the nearly fifty years since our experimental program-ming, the state's response to juvenile crime has changed beyond recognition. All the functions of the youth division have now been assumed by the Division of Family Services, and there are still some institutional programs. I have made several strong efforts to discover exactly what these programs are, and how they compare to what we were trying to do, but for reasons that escape me, I have received no response to my inquiries.

From 1960 until 1963, I worked night and day with Nelson in the key area of civil rights. I recount almost everything I did for him in those years in my chapters on marching with King and on the Rochester riots. What follows here is how he conducted himself in his work with civil rights leaders in New York during those years, while I sat at his side and learned what he did and how he did it.

Alexander Aldrich's last picture with Nelson Rockefeller in 1979 when he was Vice President.

One of the most confusing things about the civil rights movement was that the leadership consisted of a large number of charismatic people who ran the gamut between the carefully conservative who wanted gradual change, all the way to the aggressively hostile, communist-leaning radicals who wanted to change everything *now*! The challenge for Nelson always seemed to be how to interact with the people who would give him the right advice, and to avoid some of the really exploitive crazies who sometimes lurked around corners.

When I took the job in 1963, Nelson had already assembled a group of black leaders who met with him frequently, and I began to attend these meetings. They normally included Whitney Young, president of the Urban League; Roy Wilkins, head of the NAACP; and Wyatt T. Walker, pastor of the Canaan Baptist Church in Harlem, who also represented the Southern Christian Leadership Conference (SCLC).

George Fowler, the chair of the State Commission Against Discrimination (SCAD), also usually attended these meetings as my aide.

This group reflected an extraordinarily moderate, well-educated, responsible and temperate approach to racial problems at that time. The headline seekers like Adam Clayton Powell, the Harlem congressman, James Farmer, the founder of CORE, the Congress of Racial Equality, and Stokely Carmichael, the founder of SNCC (Student Non-violent Coordinating Committee) were conspicuously absent. At one point during the later days of "The Movement," SNCC began to be called the "non-student violent coordinating committee," reflecting the change in its behavior.

Nelson had been raised by his parents to pursue a life in which the prevailing prejudices about Jews, Italians, Irish, Blacks and all other minorities had no role at all. He relished these meetings with these sensitive, intelligent people who shared his values, and I know they enjoyed them as well.

I only once noticed a slight problem in those meetings, which was quickly solved. When Nelson enthusiastically agreed with somebody, he often demonstrated that by saying "Atta boy!" with a big smile and his trademark wink.

The trouble was, the term "boy" was perceived as a racial slur by almost every black man at that time. The first chance I had after I heard him use "atta boy" to Rev. Walker, I quietly warned him. From then on he would start to, and change in mid-sentence to "Aaat's the stuff!"

There was an audible sigh of relief after the first time he used the substitute phrase.

I cannot recall exactly how many of these meetings occurred, or whether any specific policies resulted from decisions made at them, but they certainly cemented Nelson's position with the moderates in the movement, and it made it easy for me to work with the minority community in my dealings as his representative.

After Dr. King's death in 1968, the moderate approach to race relations lost steam, and the movement was taken over by "Black Power" leaders like James Bevel. Strangely enough, it seemed as if King's example might have been enough to change the basic ethos of American society, and the process he began in 1963 at the Lincoln Memorial was one of the first steps to the election of Barack Obama, in spite of the efforts of both white supremacists and their black counterparts.

One of the toughest problems in a society that is founded on Judeo-Christian ethics is how to deal with people who break the law. Does our Christian God call on us to forgive the sinner? What does forgiveness mean in practice? How much should a traffic ticket cost? Should the state electrocute a man who shoots an abortionist in a church? Should we serve ham to prisoners who are Muslims?

Above all, what is the line between punishment and rehabilitation? How does society determine when someone should be released?

First as a police official, then as a juvenile rehabilitation official, and finally as an advisor to a powerful state governor, I was always perplexed by such questions, and I still am. From the time I entered police work, I made it my business to pay visits to prisons of almost every sort, both in Europe and in the United States.

I could, and if I live long enough, may some day write a book on this subject. Since this is about my relationship with Nelson, I will limit this discussion to how we disagreed about aspects of this problem.

The governor of New York State has the power to grant clemency to a criminal offender, and also to commute the death penalty if he sees fit. I once had a discussion with Nelson about this power. "I don't have very strong feelings about it," he said. "I am simply part of a statutory process, starting with the cop who arrests someone, through a cumbersome judicial procedure, then sentencing, and by the time a case comes to me and the sentence is death, the criminal has had many chances to avoid something that happens eventually to all of us."

He believed that to intervene at such a point, even if only to commute the sentence to life in prison without parole, might not represent justice

I tried arguing with him. I had submitted myself, a few weeks before this conversation, to a walk through the "last mile" at Sing Sing Prison, re-enacting what a condemned prisoner has to undergo before an execution. I had sat in the notorious electric chair. I felt that the fact that the great State of New York had a process for killing someone, no matter how justified by what that person had done, was not only grotesque, but evil and counter-productive. I tried to persuade him, but he disagreed. I even tried to suggest that he take the same walk I had, but all he said was that he would think about it (which is what he sometimes would say when he was too polite to say no). To sum up, I was never able to persuade Nelson to be more concerned with reforming the state prison system. I believe he was never persuaded that there was a strong political movement to do so, and so he simply wasn't interested, even after the disaster of the Attica Prison riots, which might have given him some public support.

17

Sing Sing

Soon after I became executive assistant to the Governor in 1960, I realized that I had no first-hand knowledge about the correctional institutions in the state, other than those run by the Division for Youth, which I had helped to create.

Accordingly, I arranged to start visiting as many of the state prisons as I could, given the crushing demands of keeping up with the governor's schedule. At the time, there were about fifteen prisons, and I remember I visited ten of them. I also visited one fascinating prison in Michigan where the inmates were taught how to play golf (!), and two prisons in California, one for men and one for women.

Visiting prisons was never my favorite pastime, although I have done it more often than most people I know. Almost all of the inmates I have met seemed to be completely normal people. For example, the young man who showed me around in Michigan pretended to be a staff member, and kept referring to "the inmates" in a dismissive manner as if he wasn't one of them (he was, for attempted murder, the warden told me later). He told me that most prisons used basketball, an all-season, mass sport, as their principal recreation; Michigan, by contrast, used golf, to teach inmates a sport they could enjoy after they were released. Sensible!

Another example was Madeline Webb, the attractive librarian at Westfield State Farm in Bedford, Westchester

173

County (later renamed Bedford Hills Correctional Facility) who was my guide there. She was a few years older than I was at the time, well spoken, educated, up-to date on world issues, and knowledgeable about state government. She also had a good sense of humor and was occasionally mildly flirtatious. Had I not known exactly who she was (due to my voracious reading of the tabloids as a chlld), I would have been charmed.

In her late teens, she had been the secret lover of an unscrupulous rogue named Eli Schonbrun. They and another man named Cullen were found guilty of murdering a wealthy, elderly Polish woman in 1943; Schonbrun and Cullen were electrocuted; Madeline was imprisoned for twenty-five years to life. She was a model prisoner, ran the library, and was paroled in 1967. She died in 1987 in Tulsa, Oklahoma.

Another of my prison adventures took place in 1964 at Sing Sing Prison in Ossining. By then, the death penalty had officially been banned by the state legislature, but was still a very hot issue. When I visited Sing Sing, the old death house was still located there, a separate prison-within-a-prison, walled off from the other prisoners, and still housing a small group of inmates who had been sentenced to death before the power to do it had been removed from the courts' jurisdiction. It also still contained the old electric chair, and the "Last Mile," the corridor where the sentenced defendant was marched to his death.

I asked the death house warden—he was a different person from the warden of the prison itself, and the most mournful-looking man I have ever met—if he would walk me through the whole process, and he agreed to. He showed me the room where the accused was fed his last meal, then the alcove where the clergy met to deliver last rites, if the accused wanted it (most of them did), then the witness room, with a clear window where newsmen sat watching the proceedings (the New York City district attorney always used to require any murder-case prosecutors to attend executions so they would realize what they were getting into). Finally, the room with the chair.

It was short, uncomfortable, dark brown and covered with restraining straps. It had a nasty looking cap hanging over its back that contained electrodes. There were also heavy metal boots into which the convicted person had to insert his or her bare feet. I dispensed with the cap and the boots, but I did sit in the chair. It was one of the grimmest things I have ever experienced.

The ghosts of the many people who had preceded me in that room have really followed me ever since. I left there with the firm conviction that I could never again support the death penalty. To me, the State of New York having a formal ritual to kill someone who might be innocent seems completely grotesque. Whenever I read of a person who has been found innocent of a crime because of DNA evidence, I remember all those men I interviewed that day on death row, each of them young and black and protesting their innocence, and I realize once again that I was right in my reaction to that awful ritual.

18

Erastus and Me

When I became Governor Nelson Rockefeller's executive assistant, there had been an Erastus Corning in office as mayor of Albany for fifty years.

Back in the dim days of 1919, a young Irishman named Dan O'Connell was elected county treasurer of Albany County. Two years later, not content with such a lowly position, he ran for chair of the Albany County Democratic Party, a position he held until his death in 1977. One of his first decisions as chairman was to select a wealthy, patrician Albanian named Erastus Corning to be the next mayor. Corning served until 1942. His son, known as Erastus II, served for the following eleven terms.

The O'Connell/Corning Machine, as it came to be called, was renowned across the whole country as one of the most corrupt, powerful urban political machines, right up there with Daley's Chicago and the old Tammany Hall in New York City.

Erastus II was a very amiable man with a most relaxed and friendly public demeanor. He wore impeccable Brooks Brothers clothes. He and Nelson Rockefeller always acted as if they had been classmates at college—warm, respectful and cozy in an exaggerated way. In fact, when they were teenagers, they had both attended an exclusive camp for boys on Maine's Mount Desert Island.

My first personal contact with Erastus II was in the fall of 1963. I had just been appointed executive assistant to the

governor, and the first call I received was from Austin Crawford, my counsel from the State Division for Youth.

The week before, the chief probation officer from Guy-
ana, South America, had arranged with me to tour New York
State's corrections agencies, escorted by Division for Youth
staff members. Two of my staff, both black, met the Guyanian
official and an aide (both also black) at Kennedy Airport and
drove him up the Hudson to Albany, visiting Sing Sing and
several other institutions on the way.

Arriving in Albany, the car stopped at an apartment
house, where one of my staff members had a girlfriend who
had invited them all for supper. Thus, an unmarked car
with four burly black men pulled into the parking lot of the
apartment building and the men went up in the elevator.
A suspicious Albany cop saw them arrive and alerted the
SWAT Team, which responded rapidly, banged on the
apartment door, and demanded the occupants open it immediately.

My staff members reacted with outrage, and they and the
distinguished international visitors were immediately carted
off to an unscheduled visit to American justice, Albany style.

They spent the night in jail.

Crawford was not only my lawyer at the youth division,
he was also chair of the Albany Chapter of the NAACP. He
was appalled at the treatment the distinguished visitors had
received!

I called Erastus Corning II's office at City Hall. He was
in Northeast Harbor, Maine, on a few days' vacation. I called
his number there and his mother answered the phone.

"Erastus is down at the dock," she said. I waited an
eternity for her to lure Erastus from the dock to the phone.

"Hello, Sam!" he boomed, "Congratulations on your
new job!"

"Thank you, mayor," I replied, "I am afraid I have bad
news."

Then I explained to him what had happened and what
I feared about the hideous news coverage that would probably ensue from this episode.

"Oh, don't worry, Sam," he said in a calm fashion.

Remembering my years in the NYPD, I had visions of a press field day, with hysterical articles and apocalyptic reactions from the U.S. State Department and the local black community, and I expressed my concern again.

"Sam," he said patiently, "When Erastus Corning says 'don't worry,' (pause) do not worry!"

"Thank you, mayor," I said, and rang off.

Five minutes later, Austin Crawford called again. "Wow!" he shouted. "They are all free, with an apology, and the press has all gone home."

I was awed by the mayor's action, and especially by his apparent power to stifle a good newspaper story. It never could have happened in New York City.

Two years later, I was sitting with Nelson in the Executive Chamber enjoying a brief conference with him. The phone rang, and it was Erastus on the line. I got up to give them privacy, but Nelson gestured for me to stay.

"Good morning, Erastus!" was the governor's greeting.

A few days before, the two had met to discuss the thorny topic of the dollar value of the streets in the South Mall. The state had condemned a large and expensive chunk of land upon which to erect the new, billion-dollar State Capitol office buildings, now named the Governor Nelson A. Rockefeller Empire State Plaza. The state Court of Claims had decided on the value of all the privately-owned land, but the value of the streets, owned by the City of Albany, was left to negotiation between the governor and the mayor. The meeting had resolved this problem, and the decision had been announced to the press.

I heard only Nelson's portion of the phone conversation.

"Oh, I'm sorry to hear that, Erastus," Nelson said. "How much would you like to settle for?"

Nelson covered the phone and with an impish grin and whispered to me, "They haven't told me yet!"

Then he turned back to the phone and said to Corning, "Well, when you've had a chance to think about it some more, you know where to find me."

It was clear that old Dan McConnell was still running the Albany machine, and that Erastus had exceeded his instructions.

The final result came a few days later, when Corning returned with a slightly higher figure, and Nelson readily agreed to it.

19

Aboard *Strider*

My first wife Elizabeth and I frequently used to cruise around Penobscot Bay, first when our boat was only a seventeen-foot lapstrake outboard with a trunk cabin named *Nimrod*, sometimes sleeping under the bow cover with out feet sticking out, and other times rowing ashore and lugging a tent.

We also would occasionally borrow my parent's boat, the *Little Wayfarer*, with its captain, Jesse Rolerson, and venture further away, usually Down East, to Mount Desert Island and beyond.

The furthest we ventured was to Roque Island on the other side of Moosebeck Reach, near Jonesport, which was as far as I could imagine going without falling off the edge of the earth. Mrs. Gardner introduced us to Captain Beale, their caretaker, who was the proud possessor of a classic Beale's Island lobster boat, the extraordinary vessel which personifies the best of Maine maritime construction, with its proud wooden tradition, its incredibly high, water-shedding bow, and the long, wide, flat stern ideal for storing high skyscraping piles of lobster pots.

I asked Captain Beale if I could ever hope to purchase such a boat for myself. He said nobody who had one would ever sell it. Then he paused and said his nephew, Willis Beale, who was nineteen, had built a splendid one for his brother the year before, and might be interested in building another one. He called Willis, who said he would.

Strider in Islesboro, Maine. Back left to right: Sam Aldrich, Phyllis Aldrich, and Taylor Watts. In front: Will Aldrich and Sarah Aldrich.

The next day, on our way home, we paid Willis a call at his barn on Beale's Island, which forms the whole southern shore of Moosebeck Reach across from Jonesport, and which was entirely populated by people named Beale or Lenfesty. Everyone there builds lobster boats, and they are reputed to marry their first cousins.

Willis made me an offer. I wanted a thirty-five-foot vessel. He offered to charge me $100 a foot for the boat and would put in a engine for what it would cost to purchase it. I had researched the subject, and ordered a 170-horse Caterpillar diesel. It cost $3,500, so we agreed that the total would be $7,000. We shook hands, and I told him I would be back the following April to take delivery.

I called him a couple of times during the winter, and each time he gave me a progress report and confirmed that he was right on time. And by April, when we returned, there was the boat. His first words were an apology: "When I set her up on the ways, it didn't look right at thirty-five feet, so I put another foot on her! I'm only charging you $3,500." She was staggeringly beautiful. I paid him in full, and ordered a couple of added wrinkles: a bow anchor winch, and a depth sounder, and I promised to return soon to take delivery.

There followed more than twenty years of blissful cruising. We named her *Strider*, after the adventurous hero of the *Lord of the Rings*, by J. R. R Tolkien, which was then our favorite book. We also had a marvelous Newfoundland dog named Frodo who fitted right in.

Every summer we moored *Strider* off our lovely summer home in Islesboro, Grindle Point. We frequently cruised on her, both east and west, sometimes alone and often with children and nieces and nephews.

On one memorable cruise with my sons Win and Alex, I brought along their first cousin, Benoni Outerbridge, It was an all-male event, and Benoni's first cruise. He was cute, very shy, and quite clumsy and unused to boats. He constantly spilled things and bumped into things, and was always saying "whoopsie" when he did. Like most boat owners, I was quite anal about the interior of the boat, and each time I heard the dreaded "whoopsie" I gritted my teeth and ran over with a sponge to clean up the peanut butter or another of Benoni's outrages.

There were two finales on the last day of the cruise. We had stopped the afternoon before to buy a real treat: a large basket of fresh Maine blueberries. I put four bowls of the delicious berries on the breakfast table, and turned to fetch a pitcher of milk, and then I heard "whoopsie!" and then a huge rattle.

Benoni had turned his entire bowl of blueberries upside down, and they were showering the bunks, the floor every cranny of the entire boat beneath.

"Nobody move!" I shouted. Without squashing any of them, I crept around and got each berry. Benoni was mortified, but I sent him out to the stern seat where he was able to finish the berries without any further damage.

Late that afternoon, on the way home to Islesboro, we were safely bound via the calm waters of Eggemoggin Reach. I decided to dump out the holding tank of the chemical toilet. I stupidly neglected to ask everyone if they might need to use it again. It was an awkward, fairly time-consuming chore, and I finished it far enough out in East Penobscot Bay so it would not foul anyone's beach. Proudly, we all arrived at our dock in Islesboro.

As we were unpacking all our gear, I made one last check below, and discovered that, as a last gift, Benoni had contributed one final "whoopsie"—he managed somehow to jam up the nautical toilet, below, and it had to be cleared again.

My first reaction was murderous, but then I realized what a wonderful story it all would be. And I forgave him. *Strider* did, too. The following day I took her out into the West Bay and dumped the toilet again. There was no lasting damage from the trip, and to my knowledge Benoni is still alive and happily married, and perhaps still saying "whoopsie."

Strider had a second life after 1971, just as I did. Two days after the blessing of our marriage in Providence, following our wedding night at the Ritz Hotel in Boston, my second wife Phyllis and I left for Islesboro, where *Strider* was waiting to take us off on our honeymoon.

The first person we met on the ferry was my first wife's brother, Harry, and as we drove off the ferry, there was Elizabeth's aunt, Sister Parish, the island's gossip, and really the last person we wanted to see. All four of us cackled with laughter at the strange coincidence.

Our honeymoon was glorious, going very far Downeast, even past Roque Island all the way to Eastport and Campobello in Canada, and thence to Grand Manan Island, ten miles out into the Bay of Fundy. I discovered that Phyllis was an avid sailor and navigator, and the best cook I had ever met. I had often been told about the forty-foot tides down there, but to experience them for the first time was a little bit the same as experiencing Phyllis for the first time. Both took a little getting used to. The first night at Grand Manan, I explored the chart carefully, and anchored in a 50-foot deep spot about a half-mile from shore. The next morning, we woke when the tide was out, in the center of a tiny circle of water with no exit until the tide had been running in for more than an hour. We went ashore that day and visited every corner of the island, high cliffs, wonderful old houses, friendly people, quaint harbors, you name it. The next night we moored to an unoccupied dolphin buoy that belonged to a fisherman who was out somewhere in the bay. I was comfortable that we would not ground out the next morning, but during the night we were hit by a truly fierce thunderstorm that made us decide to reinforce the mooring lines in the dark. Phyllis had no hesitation about how it should be done.

"You handle the engine," she said, "and I deal with the line!"

I started the engine in my pajamas and brought *Strider* up to the dolphin, while Phyllis stripped off her nightgown, grabbed a heavy nylon stern line and clawed up the side of the boat in the dark and the pelting rain, knelt on the slippery bow, bent another heavy line through the hole in the dolphin and made it fast to the bow cleat. Her seamanship and courage were both exemplary. The entire scene was brilliantly lit up every five seconds by lightning flashes accompanied by almost instant crashes of thunder. I had a dry towel ready when she reappeared.

The following day we visited the Kent Islands, a small cluster of rocks to the south of Grand Manan. We landed and discovered a party of ornithologists from the University of Maine who were searching for Leach's petrel nests along the shore. These strange birds live all their lives out of the sight of land, far out to sea. Once a year, they come to the islands, dig a burrow between the rocks, and lay a single fertilized egg. The chicks hatch, and mature underground all summer. In the early fall, before frost or snow arrives, the chicks move out at night and take off before predators can catch them. The scientists were inserting their arms into their burrows and banding the chicks so they could be traced as adults in the wild. Phyllis and I helped them for a day. It took courage and finesse to shove your arm into a hole that could easily have contained a snake, suffer being pecked by an outraged, downy chick, and then take it in hand and pull the angry little bird out into the sunlight.

We put them back, of course, encumbered by a light plastic tag on one leg, confident that they would stay there until October when they would fly away, now fully feathered, out to sea. Those that survived into adulthood would come back to the same island to lay their own eggs.

It was a magical day, and another high moment of our honeymoon. On the way home, we stopped briefly to pay a call on Willis Beale at his barn where *Strider* was created. He had seen us going by on our way Downeast the week before and was pleased that we stopped on our return trip. He was about eight years older than he had been when he built my boat, and he acted as if she were one of his children. It was a moving moment.

Returning to Islesboro was a breeze, for I was once again in familiar waters. Much of the trip was in fog, aiming successfully for a series of buoys. As we approached the south side of Mount Desert Island, we emerged suddenly from the fog and found ourselves directly opposite Nelson Rockefeller's summer home on Seal Harbor. I pointed it out to Phyllis, who chuckled and said,

"He's hard to escape, isn't he?"

From there, we returned to Islesboro and began the rest of a happy life together.

After our honeymoon and a few cruises in the Penobscot Bay area, the next big chapter in my *Strider* era mostly involved the waters of New York State, which I don't believe had ever seen an authentic Beale's Island lobster boat.

Early in the summer of 1972, I asked one of my new stepsons, Jeff Watts, to help me bring her down to Edgartown in Martha's Vineyard. He still wasn't reconciled to our marriage, but he loved boats, and I hoped it would help. I also brought along my son Alex, the old hand. The first night we got as far west as the Annisquam Canal just inside of Gloucester on Cape Ann, Massachusetts. We bunked together there overnight. The next day we crossed Massachusetts Bay on a glorious, calm, sunny day, with Boston's skyline about five miles to our starboard. At one point we passed a large pod of whales. I noticed that they would dive as we approached, and then come to the surface about four hundred feet ahead. The next time they sounded, I blasted ahead at full speed and then coasted to a stop. A few seconds later, a huge whale surfaced right next to us! He was as surprised as I was, let out a gigantic puff of air and sounded with a slap of his tail. They had had enough of us, and we went on south to the Cape Cod Canal without incident. We shot through Woods Hole on a favorable tide, with huge buoys being sucked completely under water as we went roaring by, reminding me of the whales we had seen earlier in the day. We tied up to a mooring Phyllis had arranged for us in Edgartown Harbor. We spent the rest of that week fishing for bluefish off Chappaquiddick without much luck, and preparing for the next leg of the trip. At one point I moved *Strider* down to the western side of the island, to the lovely fishing village of Menemsha. My last night on the island was spent there alone on *Strider*, so I could make an early start the next day for Montauk Point on Long Island,.

From here on, I paraphrase from *Strider*'s log, thirty-five pages of handwritten contemporaneous stuff, which is too complete for this memoir. It describes a trip that used 666 gallons of diesel fuel and a case of oil; included visits to fifty-five New York State parks and two Canadian parks; covered sixteen hundred miles of waterways; carried more than 120 passengers; and cost me $479.76. The rest of this chapter quotes from the log, identified in each instance.

I had handled *Strider* alone many times, but never out at sea, out of sight of land. It was a hot, flat, humid day, with a slow, oily swell from the Southwest. The trip to Montauk was lonely, and I was constantly aware that I had to be careful to keep a really accurate course in case the fog came in, and also never to take the slightest chance of falling overboard, even though I had taken the precaution of wearing a fat life jacket. The only company I enjoyed all day consisted of a large flock of Leach's petrels, and I amused myself for a while, wondering which of them had been plucked from their childhood lairs by Phyllis and me on our honeymoon the year before. It was a huge relief, around lunchtime to discover the southern tip of Block Island looming up dead ahead. I pulled a sandwich and some milk out of the icebox and munched past the island for the next half hour, and then maintained my westward course for the rest of the afternoon. Finally, the end of Montauk Point appeared, and I carefully rounded the point into the harbor, where Harthon ("Spud") Bill, the newly appointed regional parks administrator of the Long Island Region, joined me for a very welcome lobster dinner. From that time on I was hardly ever alone again, and I was thankful for that! The next day Spud gave me a quick tour of the Montauk Point State Park and introduced me to Perry Duryea, the state senator from Eastern Long Island who ran a huge lobster company in town. Then we headed west up Gardiner's Bay and stopped at Gardiner's Island, where we were met by its owner. My log entry reads:

> We were regaled, bullied, lectured and charmed by Robert David Lion Gardiner, 13th earl of the Manor. We toured the Oak Woods, saw the place where Captain Kidd's treasure was hidden, inspected the Hanging Tree, the graveyard, the WWII observation post, the CCC camp forest, the airstrip, and the manor itself. Also, swans, osprey, night herons, white ibis, and above all other forms of wildlife, Gardiner himself.

He wanted to persuade me to buy the place for a state park. I told him I would propose it to Nelson, which I later did. (He said no.) After three hours, we reboarded, went on through Peconic Bay, and I spent the night at Barron's Marina in Sag Harbor. Very nice! Spud joined me the next morning for the run past the Shinnecock Hills to the narrow passages that lead further west to Quogue, Center Moriches and Mastic Beach, into the Great South Bay, behind the great barrier beach of the Fire Island National Seashore, and finally

Jones Beach, our final destination of this phase of the trip. On several occasions during this voyage, I ran aground on sandbars in the middle of the well-marked channel. Apparently the channels continuously filled up, and the federal Corps of Engineers never could quite keep up with the need to dredge in a timely manner. To a person and a boat with a history of navigating in the rocky Maine coastal waters, it was an unnerving experience!

We were met at the small boat landing at Jones Beach by Hal Dyer, my assistant commissioner for administration, who had worked for me when I chaired the Taconic Park Commission. With him was Geraldine C. Welch, my special assistant in Albany. We all put on bathing suits, strolled across the beach and went swimming in the surf. Hal Dyer asked if we really were being paid to do this, and I told him that it was an approved inspection tour. The next day, Hal Dyer and I were joined by Augie Heckscher, the newly appointed New York City parks commissioner. He was a St. Paul's alumnus, a brilliant man and a great scholar of recreation and parks. I showed him his own territory of Jamaica Bay, and then we cruised together up past Coney Island, the Verrazano Bridge, my old house in Brooklyn Heights, the South Street Seaport—where we picked up Mark Lawton—the lighthouse on Ward's Island, Hellgate, and finally stopped at the new Roberto Clemente State Park near Fordham Road in The Bronx. I wish I could remember all of our conversations with Heckscher. His reminiscences about his years at St. Paul's were a large part of what he told me, and happily, they are now in a wonderful book[1] he was writing at the time. He was also interested in what Hal Dyer had to say about Mount Katahdin in Maine (where he had been chief ranger), and what I had to say about the sharks I had seen off Coney Island during my stint in the NYPD. Heckscher got off at Clemente Park, and so did Dyer and Lawton. I went on, out Spuyten Duyvil Creek and across the Hudson, where I tied *Strider* up to a

---

[1]*St. Paul's, The Life of A New England School* (New York: Charles Scribner and Sons, 1980).

transient pier at the Palisades Interstate Park Commission marina below the Palisades, where I left her for four days.

I flew to Albany, spent a day with Phyllis and the children in Greenfield Center; then back to New York and Jones Beach with Phyllis, where we attended *The King and I* at the Jones Beach Theater, and danced to Guy Lombardo's music. We slept for five hours in a motel near LaGuardia, and Phyllis flew to Albany while I went back to *Strider*. I picked up Nash Castro, superintendent of the Palisades Interstate Park Commission (PIPC), of which Laurance Rockefeller was chairman, along with a gang of newspaper people and some local officials. It was an inspiring run in a northwest breeze up the palisades, past Tarrytown, Croton Point, the Indian Point Atomic Plant, and Iona Island before we stopped for lunch at the Bear Mountain Inn.

We were an hour early, so we piled into cars and inspected Iona Island and Anthony Wayne Pool. There, I went swimming, to the delight of the cameramen. We were met at lunch by another group from the Taconic Park Commission, and cruised with them on to Norrie Point, another major boat landing north of Poughkeepsie on the east side of the river in Dutchess County,. I moored there for the night. On Wednesday, August 9, I got all the way to the Schenectady Marina on the Mohawk River! Crowded with passengers, *Strider* boldly pushed on past Catskill, Hudson, Albany, Troy and the end of tidewater at the federal Lock at North Troy. Then we returned to Waterford and the entrance to the Erie Canal.

There, waiting with her needlepoint on the edge of the old Erie Canal embankment, was Phyllis, and her sons Jeff and Taylor were scuttling happily around her. We locked through the first of the "Waterford Staircase" and said good-bye to everyone but Phyllis, Tay, Jeff, and Peter Gregory, a staff member from Albany.

The wind came on to blow really hard in the brilliant sunset, and it became a race with darkness that we lost completely. The last lock was done in total blackness and the last five miles to Schenectady was a stairway of red and white blinkers with nothing in between. We had only had the loom of land on both sides and a sputtering fathometer to guide us. Scary! At last we reached a weird succession of white hulks, which turned out to be boats tied up to wooden floats. We landed at one, and were nearly immediately joined by Mark Lawton, Chuck Cross, Gerry Costanza, her beau John Welch, and various yacht club supernumeraries. At last, at 2130 (9:30 P.M.), I could unwind and relish the goulash of peas, tunafish and onions that Phyllis prepared. Jeff and I decided to stay on the boat, while Phyllis and Taylor charged off into the darkness. What a day!

I took *Strider* up the Mohawk River twice during the 1970s, once as far as the Oswego River, thence down to Oswego, across Lake Ontario to Kingston on the St. Lawrence River, down the St. Lawrence to Sorel, Quebec, turning south up the picturesque Richelieu River into Lake Champlain. I

Strider off Fire Island in Great South Bay, N.Y., heading at full throttle for Jones Beach Marina. September, 1972. Picture by Spud Bill, regional administer, Long Island State Parks; author alone at helm.

cruised further into the Champlain-Hudson division of the Barge Canal, leaving my boat at a marina at Stillwater for the winter. That trip took an entire summer.

The second voyage, in 1973, used the entire length of the Erie Canal, from Albany to Buffalo. From there, I took a risky but enjoyable trip north down the swiftly running upper Niagara River to the small New York city of Niagara Falls. In a burst of what I remember as hubris, I had neglected to top off the fuel tanks before leaving that day.

When a diesel skipper allows his vessel to run out of fuel, there is hell to pay. The engine completely stops, develops what is called an "air lock," and can only be started again by adding substantial amounts of fuel to the tanks, and then by having the skipper manually operate a small pump on the side of the engine to remove the offending air. Then, if he is lucky, and he has pumped long enough, the electric starter will (sometimes) restart the engine.

I had a reporter from the *Niagara Gazette* on board for the trip, who later documented the event.

A few minutes after we set out, the engine died. The vessel was happily cruising downstream about four miles from the falls, and we were dead in the water. I knew we had about ten minutes before we went over the falls.

Everyone on *Strider* helped me lift the top off the engine housing in a hurry. I poured ten gallons of fuel into the offending tank, pumped furiously on the little valve on the engine's side, said a silent prayer and hit the starter. The engine roared into life. Then, almost immediately, it died.

I started pumping again, and had to perform the exercise four times before I was able to get the engine to operate long enough to get over to a float at the side of the river, and tied up to it. Safely moored, I allowed the engine to run steadily. Keith Hopkins, the Niagara Reservation State Park administrator, arrived by car from the park with a lot more fuel for me, and I was soon able to continue upstream, back to the safe premises of Buffalo.

I never again allowed *Strider* to come even close to running low on fuel.

20

A Full-time Teaching Career

I enjoyed two intense teaching experiences in my career before dedicating myself to it as a full-time professional.

My first teaching experience, which took place at City University of New York while I was secretary of the NYPD. A few years later, in 1968, I found myself teaching once again when I was recruited by Bill Zeckendorf to be the president of the Brooklyn Center of Long Island University, I insisted on teaching a graduate course in public administration for two years. The course was a delightful relief from the contentious struggles between the two wings of the faculty (deeply conservative, Catholic-educated science faculty on the right, versus radically leftist, public college graduates on the left) compounded by a totally clueless group of trustees. I was there when the shooting occurred during an anti-war demonstration at Kent State University in May of 1970. I realized that immediate action was needed, and I called a meeting of all LIU students on campus.

Without even checking with the Board of Trustees, I invited the student council to accompany me to Washington to express our concern to President Nixon. They responded handsomely, chartering a group of buses and meeting me on the mall in front of the White House the next morning, with about five hundred of their classmates. I somehow wangled a meeting with President Nixon's legal counsel,

Long Island University inauguration, 1968.

Leonard Garment, who invited the entire student council into the White House that morning. Garment was marvelous. He lived in Brooklyn Heights, was quite familiar with LIU, seemed extremely concerned with the situation at Kent State, and completely mollified my angry students. As we left the White House, the young, tough chairman of the council drew me aside and said, "Anything you want from us, Mr. President, just ask!"

I wish I could boast the same kind of success with faculty relations that I had with the students. I had inherited a long-simmering hatred between both wings of the faculty and the board of trustees, which, for years, had used tuition funds from the Brooklyn Center to support and build the C. W. Post Center in Brookville, Nassau County. The issue came to a head in the spring of 1971 when the Brooklyn Center librarian demanded a new library. I flatly opposed him; we didn't need it, and the board knew it.

The 1971 school year was to open in a faculty meeting at which an angry group of faculty, led by the librarian, planned to impeach me. I am certain I could have survived such an event, but I saved myself from embarrassment by calling the meeting to order and announcing that Governor Rockefeller had asked me to return to state service as commissioner of parks and recreation.

For many years prior to 1977, Skidmore College offered a course entitled Business Law, intended for young women who wanted to be trained in enough law that they might be qualified to serve as legal secretaries. Suddenly, in the fall of that year, instead of the usual twelve students, 160 students enrolled, all of them wanting to go on to law school later. A placid older lawyer from Saratoga Springs, Ted Grey, had taught the course for many years, and he sent out a desperate call to his friends and colleagues in the Saratoga Bar for lawyers to help him teach at least one more section of the course. I think I was the only person who agreed. We split the list of enrollees in half, and I ended up with a roster of eighty students. The largest lecture hall in Palamountain Hall was needed for each class, and I reserved it for Tuesdays and Thursdays from 8 to 9 A.M., so as not to interrupt the business day at my law firm. Ted reserved the same room for Mondays and Wednesdays during the same hour. We taught with the same textbook, which I took to Islesboro with me in August and worked out my own lesson plan, based on the chapters in the book.

I remember the students quite vividly. There was a row of brilliant Chinese girls who always sat in the front row on the right side, and had the unnerving habit of nodding in unison when they agreed with what I was saying at any time. When they disagreed or didn't understand, they would glower like a row of angry statues. Then I would explain more thoroughly my topic until I saw one or more of them nod.

It was the first year that Skidmore admitted men to the college. Three big jocks, who had been the first line of a prep-school hockey team, had applied as a group, and all had arrived that fall. They were on Skidmore's team, and sat high up on the left in my class. Generally speaking, the women that first year were far smarter and more participatory than the men. By the third year I taught, that was no longer true. It became more and more normal for bright male students to apply to Skidmore, and it really showed in classroom participation. The most memorable student in my class was Kelly Curtis, the daughter of film stars Tony Curtis and Janet Leigh, and the sister of Jamie Lee Curtis, who was not yet famous. Kelly was spectacular, five feet ten inches tall, with her father's face and her mother's figure, and as I remember, never once arrived in class on time. Her entrances always occurred about ten minutes after class began, and were designed to make the largest possible fuss. The door would open and she entered so that every eye, including my own, would follow her to take in the whole effect, which was almost always memorable.

I gave a very tough exam at the end of the course. It involved a complicated case history of a wedding party in Saratoga Springs that went completely awry: the groom's aunt got drunk and fell on the steps of the Elks Club, where the reception was held; several members of the party came down with food poisoning; the getaway car sideswiped a police car, and a few other disasters occurred. The single question, at the end, was, "Who sues whom, for what, and with what result?"

Before the exam began, I warned everyone in the classroom not to worry that this exam might seem to be very difficult, and that I intended to mark on a curve, with the best answers receiving an A. I also mentioned that classroom participation would count toward the grades. As it was a three-hour exam, I said that students could excuse themselves to use the restrooms.

A few minutes later, Kelly made her entrance and came down to the front to get her exam paper and the blue book for her answers. Within ten minutes, she came back and returned her exam paper with her blue book. Curious, I opened it. She had written a note to me: "Professor Aldrich, this exam is too hard. I refuse to answer it!"

I sat right down, using the same piece of paper, and wrote a note back to her: "Miss Curtis, had you been on time for this exam, you would have heard my message to the class [and I repeated what I had said]." Then, I continued: "I will give you one more chance. Please come to my office tomorrow morning at 8 A.M. and I will allow you to take the test again. Please act more like a grown-up the next time we meet, Miss Curtis."

My guess is that nobody had ever spoken to this young woman like that in her life. To my astonishment, she showed up five minutes early the next day, smelling of very expensive perfume and beautifully dressed. My immediate reaction was to fear that I might be accused of sexual harassment! I put her into my conference room on the first floor of my office, which adjoined my secretary's office, drew the secretary aside and asked her to watch Kelly like a hawk, and then I left.

I returned at eleven to collect her paper, which had quite a thorough answer in it. I'm happy to say I was able to give her a respectable passing grade.

A few years after graduating from Skidmore, Kelly Curtis followed her mother and younger sister into an acting career. Her credits include an appearance as Muffy in a cinematic comedy called *Trading Places*, directed by John Landis in 1983. Its stars were Dan Aykroyd, Eddie Murphy and Don Ameche. In 1991 she had a starring role in *The Devil's Daughter* wherein she played the title role in a horror movie. Her credits include many appearances in television shows and modeling assignments.

I truly wish her well.

The fall of 1976 found me at another career crossroads. I had just lost the Republican primary for the state senate, my law practice was almost nonexistent, and Nelson Rockefeller was no longer in the wings with a new job offer. An upstate senator from Plattsburgh had given me a part-time job doing research for him in his role as chair of the senate education committee, but I found out quickly it was a no-show job. I have to admit I was discouraged about my career, and I was two years shy of fifty.

Then, incredibly, I found myself on a plane from Washington, D.C., sitting next to my primary opponent, the newly credentialed State Senator Hugh Farley. For several years he had been employed by the State University at Albany as chair of the law program in the undergraduate business department. To my utter astonishment, he asked me if I would be interested in teaching in his program, holding the title of Distinguished Professor, and recruiting major political and scholarly figures to teach on campus.

I accepted without delay, and began teaching when the fall semester began. It was a very different experience from my work at Skidmore College a few years earlier. Instead of teaching about corporations and businesses, I was charged with explaining the complicated intricacies of commercial paper: checks, bills of lading, receipts, and a host of other matters that concern accountants as they track the way commerce wends its way through its myriad of paper trails. I had an incredibly complicated, and boring, textbook from which I was required to teach. I had to learn the difference between various kinds of commercial paper, and at the same time try my best to make the subject exciting to a group of undergraduates at SUNY Albany.

It wasn't until I began to compose these memoirs that I realized that the form of my life changed profoundly when I began teaching. Teaching doesn't offer the dramatic, occasionally explosive events that readers desire in a memoir. There are no Rochester Riots in commercial law, nor are there waltzes with Queen Elizabeth, or sleeping in Alabama mud next to the 82nd Airborne Division.

For five years I taught commercial law at SUNY Albany, with little out of the ordinary happening.

There was one event during those years in which I felt the kind of excitement that I remembered during my years with Nelson. I had invited the utterly unknown, young U.S. attorney from New York City, Rudy Giuliani, to come to the Albany campus as Executive in Residence to address the student body. This was his first speaking date outside New York City, and he drew a huge crowd. After I introduced him, Giuliani began speaking in a rasping, Italian whisper, in a burlesque imitation of an Mafia gangster. He was brilliant, self-deprecating, very funny, and a smashing hit. Except on television, I never saw him again after that evening, but I will never forget his performance that night.

In my fifth year of teaching at SUNY, I received an unexpected call from Bob Hawkins, the dean of the Business School at RPI, who asked me to join him for lunch. He brought along one of his top female faculty members, Jean Lynch, a leathery, profane and delightful person who was one of their best teachers, and we lunched at a well-known golf club in Loudonville where the lady in question was a famous member. The previous season, she had fractured her left wrist, and she had insisted that her orthopedist provide her with a cast that did not interfere with her golf swing. She was still wearing the cast during our lunch.

Stephen van Rensselaer, the descendant of the Dutch patroon, had founded Rensselaer Polytechnic Institute (RPI) in 1824. For many years it was the only scientific and technical institute in the English-speaking world. Its earliest alumni included Washington Roebling, the engineer of the Brooklyn Bridge, and Theodore Judah, the man who conceived and surveyed the route over the Sierras for the Central Pacific Railroad which my great-grandfather Charles Crocker built in the 1860s.

Until World War Two, RPI was the outstanding technical and scientific school in the United States. By 1945, the rise of federal research grant funding of MIT and Harvard in Cambridge, and of Berkeley and Cal Tech on the West Coast, slowly left RPI behind.

By 1970, RPI was more famous for its superb hockey team that for the quality of its students and faculty.

To its credit, the institute's board began to take intelligent steps to modernize and adapt itself to the challenges of a new era. It created a splendid new School of Management, a marvelous program to improve teaching methods for its faculty, and a Center for Urban and Environmental Studies.

The latter program was a blunt recognition of the lack of black faces on campus, either faculty members or students.

RPI named William "Doc" Zuber to come in and run the new center. He was an impatient, angry man, who lived on cigarettes and strong coffee, and who rode roughshod over the nuisances of academic bureaucracies. He must have infuriated a lot of his colleagues.

Even so, he created a program in his own image, with a small but promising group of black students who worshipped him, and who, with his support, worked hard to maintain the high academic standards of the institute.

Sadly, in 1980, Zuber's lifestyle caught up to him and he died of a heart attack. The dean of the School of Management—the only official of the institute who could cope with him—was faced with the sad task of replacing him in a hurry. And thus our lunch.

He invited me to become the new director of Urban and Environmental Studies for RPI, and I naturally assumed that I had some qualifications for the position. There was one faculty member keeping things more or less together, and of course I asked her to say on as my assistant director. Her name was Rose Dill, and she had a full-time position with the state Division for Women. In our first meeting together with Dean Hawkins, she objected to serving as "assistant" anything. I should have sensed trouble lurking, but I accepted the dean's alternative title for her: co-director. For the first couple of years, especially after I became full time, we were able to cooperate effectively. She continued in her advisory role with a number of the students for whom she was already responsible, and she continued to teach two courses at the graduate level.

Zuber had been teaching all the other courses, and I cheerfully stepped into his place in all of them. After the first exhausting year of working both at SUNY and RPI, I resigned from SUNY and began to serve full time in Troy. The teaching was a delight, both the "urban" and the "environmental" sides. The administrative side of my job slowly became an increasing hassle.

I thought I had inherited a good secretary from Zuber. She was young, black, and almost totally incompetent. Her habit was to chatter on the telephone by the hour, and I could hardly ever reach her to have her do anything for me. Discussing this with her would result in sulking appeals to Rose Dill, who was less than helpful. I finally went to Dean Hawkins, who confessed that she had not been Zuber's secretary, that she had enjoyed a poor reputation in another office in the institute, and that he had hoped she would reform if she worked for me. We replaced her without any repercussions.

A few weeks later, I noticed that the sign on the front of my office had been subtly changed. I was still listed as director.

Rose Dill's name was now listed next to mine, also designated director.

My first reaction was to laugh; I called Rose, asking if she had done it, and she admitted it. "Does that threaten you?" she bridled.

"Not a bit," I said cordially, "but you didn't agree to this, and I didn't either, and I don't want to cause any false impression about who is in charge. Let's confer with the dean about it."

Happily, Hawkins straightened her out in a hurry, the sign was changed, but I now knew Rose Dill was disloyal and had to be watched like a hawk. It didn't take too long before the next problem arose.

One of Rose's advisees was a mature black man from New York, who enrolled in the required thesis course for the Ph.D. program in the Urban and Environmental Studies Program. It was an interdisciplinary course, encompassing economics, management, some science-oriented materials, local government and statistical thinking. Each chunk of it was team-taught by faculty from other departments, including some economists, a management professor, an environmental scientist, and a statistician. It was a year-long course, with a number of challenging exams along the way, and any student who survived it could take pride in the fact that he or she had really earned the Ph.D.

It became clear after the first exam that this student was disinterested in doing any work to prepare him for the challenges involved. His answers on the test were infantile, showed no knowledge of the nature of the questions asked, and were hardly worthy of even undergraduate recognition.

Sadly, the student concerned had, only the year before, been granted a master's degree from our program, and Rose had been his advisor. I can only conclude that she had passed him because he was black, and he thought this policy would continue.

I warned him that there was no such policy, and that he had to shape up.

He didn't. He did take four more exams, failed each one, and then was appalled when he received a failing grade for the course. Having warned him repeatedly that he was in a failing situation, I was strangely unprepared for the evening when he showed up in my office in a rage. I politely sat him down in the chair next to the picture of me marching with Martin Luther King at Selma.

"You flunked me because I'm black!" he shouted.

"You flunked every test you were given in the course, each test given and graded by two professors," I coolly said. "You are entitled to appeal this grade to the dean, to the provost, and to the president of the Institute." Then I stood up, looked him in the eye and said, "This meeting is adjourned. The next time you come here, I will have my attorney present, and I advise you to bring your own." He retreated, and I never saw him again. He did appeal his grade, lost at all three levels, and that ended the matter. Was Rose Dill involved? I only suspect so. He was her advisee, and she had given him a pass as a master's student. I have a hard time imagining her hand being absent in this confrontation.

I was so busy teaching all of the courses except the two taught by Rose, traveling around to places like Medgar Evers College where able black students could be recruited, and raising enough grant money to pay the small cost of the program, that I just didn't pay much attention to her anymore.

I was busy, happy, satisfied with what I was doing, and getting very good feedback from Dean Hawkins

I started teaching at RPI as soon as I arrived there, in each of the required courses, and then, the second year, I began an honors class for graduate students in environmental regulation. I wanted to give that class a "real" experience, and so I dreamed up the idea that the City of Troy had decided to build a boat landing on the banks of the Hudson River, and our class had been hired as consultants to do all the studies necessary to achieve the goal.

Incredibly, the first student who called the appropriate official at Troy City Hall was informed that the city was indeed planning to build such a boat landing, and that they would be most interested in having RPI do some of their work for them!

The city's Public Works Department was the coordinating agency. They needed approval from the Federal Corps of Engineers, which had jurisdiction over traffic on the river: from the state, which had title to the riverbed; from the County of Rensselaer, and from several city agencies, including the Zoning Board and the Zoning Board of Appeals. As with every other project, they had to communicate with various utilities, such as the telephone company and Niagara Mohawk.

I arranged for the students to prepare the first drafts of all these papers, to perform any research that might have to be done to get all of this prepared, and to oversee the submission of many of these documents.

Everything went through perfectly. Late the following spring, the mayor announced that the new boat landing would be opened on the Fourth of July with an appropriate celebration. I prepared a list of the students involved, assuming all of them (and I) might be invited to the event, and perhaps acknowledged for their contribution.

No such luck! We were never invited, no mention was made of the hours of work that RPI students had done to help, nothing!

"No class Troy?"

Although that experience was frustrating, all of the other contacts I had at RPI were fulfilling and positive for seven years, especially taking the course one faculty member gave, on how to be an effective teacher, which no other college gives, to my knowledge.

Then the ax fell.

RPI's president retired, and a new candidate was selected. His name was Byron Pipes, then serving as president of the University of Delaware. Before even arriving on campus, he announced that his intention was to discharge every faculty member who was not tenured.

I was far too loyal to the program I had rescued and recreated to accept such a stupid and mindless statement. I immediately appealed it to the author, sending him a respectfully persuasive letter about the need for such a program, and that it was self-supporting. I never got a reply, other then a memo from the provost that said the president was adamant. In short, I was sacked!

I only had three satisfactions after this shock. The first was that the provost, whom I had never admired, was the second officer fired in the bloodbath. The second was that, within two years, Pipes himself was canned by the institute's trustees. The third was that, also within two years, I had been hired in a similar position by SUNY Empire State College, and my personal commute was shortened from an hour by car to a five-minute walk.

Tenure be damned!

After my unceremonious dumping at RPI, I applied for a full-time faculty position at SUNY Empire State College's Center for Distance Learning (CDL) in Saratoga Springs. The job description wasn't exactly what I wanted but, after some negotiation the school redrafted it and I was hired as professor of Public Policy Studies, which included a number of academic areas I had not handled at RPI but which suited me fine, such as fire control management.

To my delight, the new position was located at One Union Avenue, a short walk from my home. The salary and benefits were comparable to what I had been receiving. My new boss was a truly splendid fellow named Dan Granger, who was most supportive and who really helped me in every way. Every other morning, we worked out together in the YMCA pool nearby, a drill that made our relationship even closer. I could scarcely believe my good fortune.

Empire State College had clearly adopted the *persona* of its founder, Jim Hall, and was extremely open, friendly to new approaches, and experimental. The same was even truer for CDL, and I found I had to work hard to adapt to teaching by mail and the internet. I had young male students from Hawaii, single moms from Western Pennsylvania who did their homework after putting their children to bed, and a young fireman from Ohio who wanted to become a deputy chief in their department, and so on.

I have never enjoyed myself more.

Once a year, at college commencement ceremonies, usually in June, faculties get a chance to parade in their academic robes, most of which are black. In recent years, trends have allowed undergraduates to change this grim tradition, sometimes substituting pale blue or white.

For faculty, universities years ago began substituting much more vivid colors for the robes of their alumni. I am entitled to wear the Harvard JD robe, which is a vivid crimson, with purple piping on the black collar. I wore this for the commencement at Long Island University in June, 1970, when the temperature and humidity were both out of sight.

The only problem seemed to be the almost constantly expanding student caseload. I was there for seven years, and it never seemed to ease off, even in the summer. I gradually became exhausted.

Once again, I don't think teaching lends itself to memoir treatment, because of its repetitive nature. However, there were two occasions when students whom I had never met except "on line" actually came by physically to meet me and thank me for my assistance. One was a single mom from Pennsylvania who arrived one day at my office to give me a hug; and the other was a young man from the Capital District who asked to speak at his graduation, during which he reported how much my help had meant to him. These two events were of great significance to me!

On several occasions I visited the National Fire Academy in Emmetsburg, Maryland. This was because our program had been assigned the job of delivering distance learning credits to their students who desired to take them from us. I had to attend an unpleasant meeting in which a representative of the Clinton administration gave us the unwelcome news that they had decided to discontinue our role. I demanded to know why such a decision had been made, and she glibly replied that the decision had been to privatize the program, and we should be happy about it!

I left that meeting determined to use every skill I had ever learned in public life to change that decision, by communicating personally to each congressman on the Firemen's Caucus, including my old Harvard classmate Amory Houghton, Jr., and Charlie Rangel, the chair of the House Ways and Means Committee and my friend from the Selma March. My appeals fell on deaf ears.

I loved those seven years, nevertheless. I shared an office with Frank Quinn, who became a wonderful friend, and hugely admired the two directors of the program I worked under: Dan Granger and Meg Benke. They were inspiring bosses.

I would still be there but for the stroke, which flattened me on my way to work in 1999.

21

Phyllis

We first met at the lighthouse picnic in Islesboro in August 1969. She was there visiting her first husband's mother with her children. Despite her recent divorce from their father, she was still on the most cordial terms with his mother, a condition that continued for the rest of the older woman's very long life. Phyllis hadn't wanted to attend the party, but I remember to this day meeting for the first time such a wonderfully attractive, interesting, intelligent, energetic, passionate and sympathetic woman. I asked her where she was staying, and she mentioned a farm on the west shore up the island. I offered to give her a ride home on my boat, *Strider*. She smilingly pointed out there was no dock there. I gallantly offered to tow a dinghy and row her ashore. Laughing, she said her mother-in-law was bringing her home. But I vowed I would never forget her.

That fall, I went to work for Long Island University in Brooklyn, and moved with Elizabeth into an apartment on Pierrepont Street. The dissolution of our marriage was well along, but she moved into the apartment with me and helped to arrange the acquisition of the necessary furniture. Our oldest children were away at school, but Amanda and Alexander were entered at Packer and at St. Ann's School, respectively.

One of my first actions was to set up a performing arts program for LIU. Thinking I might need an aide to help

Picture of Phyllis, taken in Brooklyn by Judy Brown, her best friend. We got married a few weeks later.

coordinate the program, I advertised a position. It was, of course, a full-time job. Incredibly, the first person to apply was a young woman who lived nearby named Phyllis Watts, who sent me her resumé. She was a teacher at St. Ann's School, and was the same woman I had met at the lighthouse the year before!

I soberly interviewed her for the job at my office in the old Paramount Theater building on Flatbush Avenue. I offered her the job on the spot.

Two days later, she turned me down. With three little children to support, and with all three enrolled tuition-free at

St. Ann's where she taught third grade, working at LIU made no sense to her. She had to be home for them after school, and the LIU job involved many evenings at the college.

I was staggered, but determined to see her again.

Several months later, Elizabeth left me for good, leaving Brooklyn to establish residence in Idaho, to obtain a divorce terminating twenty years of marriage. Under more normal circumstances I would have been devastated. But some instinct told me that my life was just about to begin.

And it did.

I won't describe our courtship in detail. I think, in retrospect, that Phyllis and I should have been a little slower about it, so our children and friends would have had more of a chance to get used to the idea. But there is no real manual about how to behave when you are smitten with the kind of love I felt, and I wanted to pursue her quickly so she would have no opportunity to meet another man who could take her away and destroy the happiness I had just found.

The first occasion we had to get away was the first day of spring vacation at St. Ann's, when we stole off for a long weekend on the Outer Banks of North Carolina. The weather was glorious with an enormous full moon at night, and we discovered that nobody had ever been as much in love as we were. We began, slowly, to introduce our children to each other.

In June 1971, I decided to remove some of the uncertainty. I arranged a visit to Islesboro for all of us. Moving seven curious children to Maine for a long weekend was challenging, but it gave me the chance to spirit Phyllis out to the sunken garden, place her on the stone wall, and humbly ask for her hand in marriage. She said "OK," thereby making me the happiest man in Waldo County.

Then, of course, I had to survive meeting and gaining the blessings of each of her four sisters, which required a visit to each of them, and to Uncle Bill Hoyt, and to her father and stepmother. Happily, her entire family was almost as wonderful as she was, although two of her sisters were suspicious of my intentions and protective of her. Her father,

Clem Williamson, was the most enthusiastic of men, a lot like Phyllis. Although a Yale man and a staunch Goldwater supporter, he totally accepted the fact that I was a Harvard man and a Rockefeller supporter, and said, if Phyllis wanted me, that was enough for him.

My own father was not so easy. I am convinced that he got it into his head that Phyllis wasn't socially prominent enough, and so he didn't trust my judgment about her. That ridiculous attitude was torpedoed in a totally unexpected way at the blessing of our marriage in late July.

Because my own divorce from Elizabeth had only become final in June, the Episcopal Church refused to marry us when we wanted. Accordingly, I persuaded my former police department colleague Bob Mangum to marry us. By then he was a court of claims judge in New York City, with a license to perform marriages, and he was thrilled to do it. We were quietly married in a dignified civil ceremony in Judge Mangum's chambers at 270 Broadway in New York, before two witnesses: Judy Brown and Bill Stackpole.

We needed a fairly large place in Providence to celebrate the Episcopal blessing of the marriage, and the logical place would have been the ancestral home of the Aldrich clan on Benevolent Street, which my father then occupied. I suggested the idea to him, but he grumpily said it would not be appropriate, thus endearing him to me forever. Instead, the blessing took place at Phyllis's father Clem Williamson's house nearby on Cushing Street. All our children were there, and almost all our combined families: three of my sisters, and all four of hers. The high moment was the arrival of John Nicholas Brown and his formidable wife, Ann. They were the nicest, richest, and most socially prominent couple in Providence, a pair that my father worshipped and admired in almost every way. Their daughter Angela had been Phyllis's roommate at Radcliffe for four years.

When the Browns walked in, my father hurried forward to welcome them. They brushed him aside, and pounced on Phyllis. Mr. Brown took her into his arms, looked up at my father, who looked stunned, and said: "Alexander is the luckiest man in the world!"

The Reverend Ben Williams, from Christ Church in Islesboro, then took over, and the blessing took place in a wonderfully spiritual way. A warm and marvelous party ensued, with Judy Brown taking a lot of photographs. When it was over, Phyllis and I drove away in a limo to Boston to start our honeymoon on *Strider*, and my oldest daughter Elizabeth drove all the other children back to New York.

Complicated, yes, but we were at last together, and married forever.

The promises Phyllis and I made at our wedding thirty-nine years ago have been fulfilled in every possible way. I have happily watched her grow and discover herself as a teacher, administrator, mother of two of my children, guide and mentor for me, perceptive and loving stepmother, ocean sailor, gourmet cook, hostess, flower and vegetable gardener, beef cattle farmer, lover of the arts, conversationalist, voracious reader and scholar, loving grandmother to eighteen glorious grandchildren, travel agent, house designer, builder and clerk-of-the works, doctor, nurse and emergency chauffeur (when I had my stroke) and, most recently, the brave survivor of a kidney transplant while serving our church in a key role in selecting a new pastor, and founding an Episcopal school in our parish. Her passion for life is undiminished. And she remains as modest as ever.

My love for her continues to grow and flower. There are many mornings I wake up wondering what I ever did to deserve such a wonderful wife.

We discovered about three years after our wedding that she had inherited the polycystic gene which had killed her own mother at the age of forty-nine.

On my annual excursion to Egypt in 1976 to attend the annual meeting of the American University in Cairo, the board of trustees was invited to attend the dedication of its new Desert Development Center near Sadat City, a few miles from Cairo. I went, of course, and found myself at lunch, sitting next to a very interesting lady, an employee of a small American foundation from which the university was hoping to receive a contribution. Her name was Betsy Combier, and she came from New York.

Strangely, the only Combier I had ever heard of was P. Hodges Combier, a nit-picking assistant attorney general in Albany, who had driven David McGovern crazy some ten years before. I asked her if they were related, and she told me that he was her father, but totally estranged from her and her mother.

At that point, she inquired if I was married, and I told her that I was, very happily so, and very recently.

To my astonishment, she asked: "So what's the problem?"

Somehow, she had picked up some vibes from me.

"The only problem is that we recently learned that my wife has polycystic kidneys, a disease that killed her mother at age forty-nine," I said, "and I am very worried about her."

She examined me with speculative eyes, and then said, "It seems to me that you are a healer, and that you might be able to heal her disease or greatly delay its arrival!"

"How do I do that?" I said.

"Like any other healer does," she cried. "By laying on of hands!" I was slightly stunned.

Our paths crossed only once more, on the Lexington Avenue Subway, a few months later. She was across the car, on the uptown local, and we got off at the same stop. I followed up the stairs, called out to her, and her first words were: "How is Phyllis?" I told her I was following her advice, trying to heal her, but without telling her what I was doing.

"Keep it up!" she said.

I did, for a long time not telling Phyllis, but for year after year, after we went to bed at night, I would gently lay my hand on her back, roughly where I imagined her kidneys might be located, and simply allow it to rest there. Sometimes I would focus very hard, but most of the time I would simply rest there until I went to sleep.

Did it make any difference?

I have two reasons to think it might have. For one thing, as I write this, she is in her seventies, more than twenty years older than her mother was when she died. For another, we have recently discovered that there is a school of thought, actively being practiced in Hartford, that pursues renal health through the laying on of hands. Interestingly enough, they think that the procedure is related to dowsing.

Sadly, shortly after I wrote the last paragraph, her renal physician discovered that her kidney efficiency had declined to about five percent, and it soon became necessary to have a transplant or dialysis.

Phyllis continued her vigorous lifestyle while searching for the best place to achieve these goals. We quickly narrowed the choices to three hospitals: Johns Hopkins in Baltimore, Columbia Presbyterian in New York City, and Albany Medical Center. The latter two had staff members who had been trained at Johns Hopkins, where Phyllis' sister, Cynthia Fulton, had received one of her two transplants.

Gwynneth, Sharon, Sunny, Cynthia, and Phyllis.

In the early spring of 2008, Phyllis arranged to fly to Virginia to attend an educational conference. Her physician at Albany Med, Dr. Conti, called me on the phone and asked for her. I informed him she was about to get on a plane at the airport.

"We have a kidney that is an exact match for her!" he yelled.

I gave him her cell phone number.

He reached her as she was handing her boarding pass to the agent. She took the pass back, got her bags, and went straight to Albany Med to be evaluated. The following morning she became the proud possessor of a healthy kidney from a thirteen-year-old girl who had been killed in a car crash.

Dr. Conti told us that it had been a miracle that they had found an exact match for Phyllis so soon, and although the first year was a rocky period for her recovery, punctuated by four hospitalizations—two of which kept her away from my own eightieth birthday celebrations—she is today thriving, busier than ever, and serving as the principal of the new school at St. George's Church, Clifton Park.

My greatest challenge with Phyllis is simply keeping up with her.

22

A Farmer's Life for Me?

Except for a couple of months stringing miles of barbed wire fence for a King Ranch in Idaho one summer while still a teenager, I had no experience in cattle farming until my wife and I quite literally "bought the farm."

In 1971 I left Brooklyn Heights, returning to Upstate New York with a new job as state park commissioner, urgently needing to find a house large enough to hold my energetic new wife and the seven children we brought into our marriage. I wanted to be within commuting distance of Albany, and not too far from the Saratoga Spa State Park, the crown jewel of the park system.

I asked county Republican chairman Jim Foley for the name of a reputable realtor, and he recommended a well-known Republican. In my usual, impulsive way, I went to the yellow pages with the man's last name and found the name of his brother, who was also in real estate. Years later I found out I had contacted the "wrong" brother, politically, but he found me a wonderful place that was just the right size, fairly inexpensive, with a huge cow barn, a milk shed, a pond, and 250 acres of wonderful land, both open and forested.

It belonged to Harold L. Hall, who had just retired from the dairy business and moved across the road, and he offered to throw in thirteen prime white-faced Hereford cows with the deal. Was I interested?

Author with our only charolais cow about 1975. Picture by Phyllis Aldrich.

Phyllis and I conferred at great length, encouraged by Harold's offer to help us, and we decided to go for it. We had wonderful visions of organic food, a huge vegetable garden, and relying on our children to help out, the way farm kids everywhere do. I bought most of Harold's equipment, including three hay wagons, two old International Harvestor tractors, and a Cub Cadet lawn tractor for mowing the grass around the house. At Harold's recommendation, I also invested in a new mower/tedder, a large diesel tractor that had the power to operate the new equipment with something to spare, with snow-plow, shovel and log-splitter attachments.

My last purchase was a handsome Black Angus bull. I should have bought a white-faced Hereford, for he would have matched the cows and their progeny would have marketed more readily, but I thought all I was interested in was meat, and someone had told me that Angus tasted better. What did I know?

We started our farming adventure the following spring when I brought Phyllis and her three Watts children up from Brooklyn. For her and for me, it was a wonderful adventure; for the kids, fresh from the streets of Brooklyn and the shelter of St. Ann's School, it must have been a serious culture shock. Our house on Wilton Road in the Town of Greenfield, was surrounded by Harold Hall descendents, Davises and Halls, who must have considered the Watts children and the Aldriches to be exotic creatures from a distant planet. To everyone's credit, especially the Davises, we were welcomed and helped on a daily basis. When it came time to bring in the hay, we all shared the mowing, the raking, and the baling, and the back-breaking task of piling the hay in the haymow in the barn.

How well I remember sweating out the days between mowing the grass, and hoping for dry, hot weather so the hay would cure enough for us to bale it. It always seemed to start thundering by the end of the second day, threatening to destroy a whole crop before we could throw the dry bales into the wagons and race them under cover before the rain came down.

The barn was colossal—at that time the largest single agricultural structure in the whole county. One summer we harvested and stored a solid sixteen thousand bales. There were two holes in the floor of the haymow. All winter long, every morning, I would climb up and throw down enough hay for the cows and the bull to consume during the rest of the day.

Phyllis decided that her children should have their own animals to tend. Cynthia wanted her own horse, and this translated into her being in charge of all the family's horses, at one time amounting to five animals. Jeffrey wanted, and got, a huge female pig, and developed a wonderfully intense ambition to make money, breeding out an annual gang of piglets. The sow's name was Homer, and she had the unfortunate habit of rolling in her sleep and squashing her piglets and Jeffrey's profits.

Taylor kept chickens, which provided us with fresh eggs.

Phyllis herself concentrated on a large and productive vegetable garden just across the creek from the kitchen door.

She spent hours there on her hands and knees, totally happy with her planting, raking, weeding, and harvesting. She lugged in baskets of wonderful potatoes, broccoli, pumpkins, peas, beans, carrots, zucchini, sweet corn, and other organic products. Before the end of the first year, I gave her a shiny red Troy-bilt rototiller which became her most prized possession. Every spring from then on, I spread a layer of rotted cow manure on the garden, ground it all into the soil, and then staked out a grid of string on the ground, so she could lay out orderly rows of seeds and seedlings. Sadly, she was never able to follow the strings properly, so her rows always ended up looking like the wakes of a sailing vessel, drunkenly tacking downwind. I never complained, because the food was always so delicious.

The bull proved to be a prodigious breeder. The first summer he impregnated thirteen cows, who proceeded to deliver fourteen healthy calves the following spring. The twins turned out to be a male and a female. I discovered a whole new term to enrich my life: "freemantle!" This is the term that describes a male whose masculine genes are overwhelmed by the female genes of his twin sister in the womb. The resulting male calf is sterile and puny, and quite useless as breeding stock.

Regardless, we had five splendid male calves, which we sold as steers the following autumn at the Argyle Auction in Washington County. They fetched about $400 apiece, a great disappointment. This turned out to be the only income we would earn from the farm, and I soon understood the grim economic future of our experiment in agribusiness.

Both Phyllis and I had full-time jobs while we lived on the farm, but we never had a farm manager. When problems arose, we handled them ourselves as best we could.

We learned to deal with *Fences Breaking*. Angus cows are notorious "leaners." To be specific, they are prone to lean against fences, perhaps to scratch themselves. The result is frequent ruptures in the fence lines, followed by the arrival of the whole herd on the road or on the neighbors' property. Normally this would occur when I was away in Albany or

New York City, and Phyllis had to answer an anguished call while at a faculty meeting at Skidmore, rush home, herd the cows back in, and repair the fence. Just once it was my responsibility, at a time when I had planned to go away but had changed my plans because of the weather. Of course, I didn't notify the cattle, and they broke out. That day, I had to gather them up and fix the fence myself.

The Olympic Cow. Only one of our cows was truly athletic. Now and then we were puzzled by finding her all alone, bellowing pathetically outside the gate. Later our babysitter spotted her gracefully leaping the fence at a low place.

Water Pipes Freezing. The barn was fully equipped with water bowls and heating tape, so the cows could drink in all weather. The system never worked properly in below zero weather, however. Pipes split, and I became an electrician, pipefitter, and cusser.

Calf Birthing: Every spring I found a few cows in the field, heaving away, with two legs protruding out of their hind end. I learned from Harold Hall that the remedy was to grab, pull down, and stand back. It always worked. A calf—and once, two calves—came gushing out.

Manure Spreading: Once a week, usually Sunday, I ran the diesel tractor into the barn and brought out all the manure piled up on the floor. I dumped it into a large spreader, where it would rot for a few days, and then I would spread it on the fields or on Phyllis's garden.

Castration Assistance: Doc Hansen, our vet, dropped by each year to neuter our new calves. It was a job I could not bring myself to perform, but I felt constrained to assist him by holding the calf while the operation was done.

Bringing In the Hay: We had a lush supply of grass on our acreage that came up each year without prompting. All we had to do was to mow it, allow it to dry, rake it, bale it, and finally stow the bales in the barn. All we ever needed was five uninterrupted days of sunny weather in June! *Ha!* Our tax accountant in those days was a fellow Rotarian, George Walker, who gave us the Good News that the law allowed us to amortize capital expenditures for the farm, and also to deduct operating expenses from our adjusted gross income. The Bad News was that this arrangement would only last for the first seven years. It became very clear to us, in a few short years, that the more cattle we bred, the more money we would lose on the farm, and we could no longer deduct those losses. By 1978 we would have to give up farming.

As our children grew up and went off to boarding school we sold the horses, the pig and the chickens. Then in one great spasm, we auctioned off the cows and the bull, and all the machinery. One of the last agricultural things I did was to bring the spreader to 104 Union Avenue in Saratoga Springs, to apply a final huge layer of manure to Phyllis's garden at our new city house.

Do I miss farming? Yes, very much. It was a wonderful lifestyle for a vigorous young family. Staying fit was not a problem. Each child had an important discipline. The food was amazing; we ate everything we produced. The best thing of all was going out to the barn at dawn to feed the cattle. The whole herd would bellow a grateful welcome to me, as I scrambled up to the loft to throw down their bales.

There are a few things I don't miss at all: rainfall during hay season in June; repairing machinery and barn plumbing in below-zero temperatures; realizing that the small family farm is a luxury in today's economy, and waiting for the financial axe to fall.

The federal Historic Preservation Act of 1975 provided that state actions involving federal assistance, such as certain stated road projects, were subject to review by the National Advisory Council on Historic Preservation if the project might impose a threat to a historic site. President Gerald Ford appointed me as a member of the ACHP a year later.

In the early winter of 1977, ACHP Director Robert Garvey called me from Washington and asked me to reserve time the following week to sit in on a meeting of his staff to examine a tough little case in Troy, where the state Department of Transportation intended to build a new bridge across the Hudson River, carrying Route 7 across the Hudson to its intersection with the Adirondack Northway. The design of the approach to the bridge on the Troy side was so drafted that it neatly removed about four feet from the southwest corner of the Esek Bussey Firehouse, a building of no particular importance except that it was one of the last remaining examples of nineteenth-century firehouse architecture in that city. The local preservationists were furious, the highway people were immovable, and it looked as if the building had to be torn down. The ACHP was called in to mediate, or call a public hearing, which would delay the whole project.

I agreed to go.

The morning of the meeting dawned at twenty-seven degrees below zero. As I was accustomed, I went out to the barn to feed the cows. At the time we had eighty-nine animals on our farm, so many that I had placed a big steel feed wagon outside the main barn and filled it so that cows who couldn't crowd inside could have access to feed. First, I threw down about fifty bales from the haymow to the feed racks, and then I went out into the yard to check the wagon. There I found that one of our largest cows had somehow slipped under one end of the hay wagon, and was bellowing in distress.

I ran back to the house and called our veterinarian, Doc Hansen, the only doctor in Saratoga County who still made house calls, and asked him to come, quick. He replied that he had a dozen calls already, and gave me the bad news that by the time he could arrive, the cow would already be dead. It seems that when a cow is held in a prone position it cannot burp, slowly fills with gas, and will die unless it is immediately pulled up. He gave me clear instructions as to what to do, and I followed them.

Diesel fuel is reluctant to flow at twenty-seven below, but I had to get our tractor to work. I had plugged in its heater the night before, so it actually started. Then I had to get a thin chain around the hindquarters of the cow. Next I had to maneuver the tractor around the cow and the wagon, hook the tractor to the tongue of the wagon, and somehow pull and push the wagon so I could unhook it and come around to hook the bucket to the chain and lift the cow's butt up into the air. Per instructions, I dropped the bucket, the chain fell off, the cow emitted a cosmic burp, and without a word of thanks went trotting away.

At that point I looked at my watch, and realized that the meeting was about to start.

I parked the tractor, plugged the heater in, and ran at top speed back to the house. There stood my lovely but house-defending wife, firmly demanding that I drop all my outer clothes into our washing machine. I showered, got into a business suit, grabbed my briefcase and headed for Troy, my overcoat in the back seat.

The trip should have taken an hour, but in forty minutes I arrived at the firehouse. I apologized for keeping them all waiting and made them listen to the whole story as I have just related it. They were more tolerant than I would have been, to be sure.

And what happened to the Esek Bussey Firehouse?

Sadly, neither the historians nor the highway engineers could agree on a compromise, such as moving the design five feet to the south. The matter went to a full hearing before the ACHP, which recommended that the building be saved. Then the engineers listened, and I am proud to say that the design was changed, and the firehouse still stands today.

I fear I can't say the same for the cow.

23

Fatherly Farewell

In late August of 1972, my father quite suddenly announced his intention to charter a yacht and cruise up the Hudson and Mohawk rivers. He asked me to come with him and be his guide. Winthrop Aldrich was eighty-six years old at the time and pretty cranky, but I was thrilled and accepted his invitation enthusiastically.

I had never felt that I met my father's expectations, and our relationship had been somewhat distant and difficult. Former ambassador to Great Britain and chairman of the Chase Bank, he had wanted me to follow in his footsteps. Instead, I found my own path.

This trip was important to us both, and I decided to orchestrate the journey around a few visits with some distinguished upstate local leaders who were chairmen of regional state park commissions, hoping to show my father a bit about my functions as commissioner of New York State parks.

I met my father at the marina in Catskill Creek. His chartered vessel was a sixty-foot yacht with two diesel engines and so beamy I had severe doubts about its ability to fit into any of the locks on the way up the Mohawk. A full-time crew of two men, a captain and an engineer, was required to handle this behemoth, and the captain doubled as the chef while in port. We spent the night on board the boat, in complete luxury in separate cabins. The engineer made our bunks while the captain gave us breakfast.

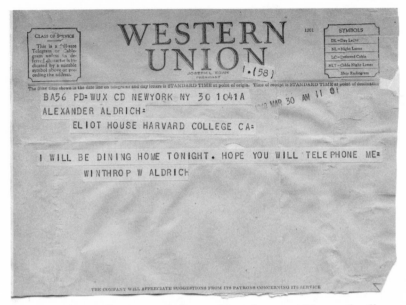

Telegram from affectionate father to his only son at Harvard college, March 30, 1947. Clearly composed by Minna Frank, secretary to the Chairman of the Board, Chase National Bank. Brrrr!

I had my state car pick us up the next morning to visit Olana, the Hudson River School artist Frederic Church's fantastic mansion overlooking Catskill. In 1966 I had been extremely active in the local effort to save Olana from developers. It was now a state park. I showed him around, but he was not impressed. We had gotten off to a bad start.

We returned to Catskill, from whence we went boiling up the Hudson on a strong fair tide. I regaled my father with tales of my years with the Hudson River Valley Commission, showed him the Hudson Lighthouse, told him that Hudson had been a whaling port during the War of 1812, and treated him with views of various Livingston and Clinton houses along the way. He began to warm up a little. Passing Albany, he got very interested when I pointed out what Nelson Rockefeller, his nephew, was doing with the South Mall project. I had forgotten that my father had been counsel to Rockefeller

Center when Nelson was building it. I got him talking about those years, and he warmed up some more.

We finally arrived at the locks at Waterford, and as we pulled into Lock Number 1, right under the sign saying "TO BUFFALO 280 MILES," was my wife, Phyllis, radiant and eight months pregnant with our son, William C. Aldrich.

After we had entered the lock, Phyllis happily climbed aboard and gave my father a warm hug. He appeared to be quite alarmed, and I suddenly realized he thought she could easily go into labor on the boat, especially if he had hugged her back. We had to reassure him that this was extremely unlikely, that the child wasn't expected until October and that Phyllis was an experienced hand on a boat and could take

Picture of William C. Aldrich as a "Mite" hockey player in Saratoga Springs at the age of four; 1977. Picture by author. "DAD, IT'S SLIPPERY!" he said.

care of herself handily. Even so, he grumpily announced that Clarence Dillon had died on this boat earlier in the summer, and he did not want to have someone born on it right away. His attitude was hostile and unfeeling, and hardly made Phyllis feel welcome at all.

He was visibly relieved when I told him she was only staying until we arrived in the Mohawk.

That evening I drove her back to Greenfield, and rejoined my father at the Schenectady Marina the next morning. After reassuring him that Phyllis hadn't begun labor yet, we slowly cruised on to Fonda/Fultonville where we were met by the chair of Saratoga-Capital District Regional Park Commission, William St. Thomas, a Gloversville leather manufacturer. Bill was an interesting man with a huge ego, and very proud of his social standing in the Mohawk Valley and of his friendship with Nelson Rockefeller. He immediately hit it off with my father, and I was happy to hear him say how helpful I had been to him in running all the parks in his region. I quietly chuckled at this gentle exaggeration; before Nelson had centralized the entire system under me, each of the chairs had a lot of responsibility for day-to-day management. They still held meetings, but any desired commission changes were advisory to me.

I later explained this to my father, who for the first time realized I had a very big job on my hands.

The next big event was the arrival of the chair of the Finger Lakes Regional Commission, Alan Treman, distinguished professor at Cornell. He met us at Brewerton, at the western end of Oneida Lake, where the Erie Canal meets the Oswego River, which empties into Lake Ontario. I had recently dedicated the lock as a state park, and Treman hadn't seen it yet.

He was almost as impressed with what we had done with the lock and its surroundings as he was with meeting my father. Treman was a noble looking man, tall and handsome, already in his seventies, very courteous to both of the Aldriches, and he outdid Bill St. Thomas in telling my father how important I was to the park system.

We went on down the river to Fort Oswego, a restored French and Indian War fortress at the edge of Lake Ontario. Our next stop was to be Alexandria Bay at the start of the St. Lawrence River. To my father's fury, the engineer announced that his sister was sick, and that he had to leave immediately. The captain of the boat tried to persuade my father that he could do it all, but my father said the charter had been breached, and that the cruise was over!

Finally, they agreed to a compromise. The captain agreed to serve as engineer, and my father and I would take turns at the helm. We headed glumly out onto Lake Ontario. I navigated, my father steered, and the Captain sat below, watching the dials in the engine room.

Catherine Johnson, chairwoman of the Thousand Island Regional Park Commission and wife of John B. Johnson, publisher of the *Watertown Times*, met us there. They were both attractive, much younger than either St. Thomas or Treman, and delighted to see both of us. My father had cooled down, did his best to be charming, and the Johnsons were delightful guests.

I had hoped to show the old man the St. Lawrence River and all the neat parks on both the New York and Canadian sides. Sadly, he decided that the strain of our journey was getting to him, and he decided to terminate the charter and take the next plane back to New York. With some relief, I agreed and got the state plane to fly me back to Albany.

Sadly, when he got back, my father's doctor diagnosed prostate cancer, requiring surgery.

He died a little more than a year later.

Before his death, I returned to his bedside at Presbyterian Hospital. He was pathetically weak when I appeared. His final words to me were, "This is going to cramp my style terribly!"

I would have preferred him to say something nice about our trip, but that was not his way. I had to be satisfied that he came at all, and that he heard my professional colleagues say some nice things about me.

24

Parks Commissioner

My return to Albany from Long Island University in the fall of 1971 occurred at a pretty grim time for New York State. The bloody suppression of the Attica Prison riot had just occurred on September 13. This was followed on the 17th by a Weathermen-sponsored explosion in the men's room in the Corrections Department headquarters in Albany.

I arrived that day and was greeted with the news that I had to arrange to move the Parks Department office out of its home at Building 2 at the State Campus to an unfinished chunk of the huge Motor Vehicles Building at the South Mall complex. This proved to be an extremely unpopular idea with my newly acquired staff, because of downtown parking problems but, for security reasons, Building 2 was the ideal place to put Corrections, and I had no choice at all.

Our new offices were prepared in about a week, and we moved in immediately. I later found out that the only changes were to slip in a bathroom with shower next to the large office at one end to accommodate the new commissioner. Every department head in the state is entitled to such a perk, and so I was never consulted on the decision. After I occupied the place, one of my children presented me with a Snoopy bath towel to place in the new facility, but I don't ever remember showering there.

Author's swearing in as Parks Commissioner, 1971. Front row: Jeffrey Watts, Taylor Watts, Cynthia Watts; middle row: Governor Rockefeller, Alex Aldrich, author, Phyllis Aldrich; back row: Laurance Rockefeller (behind Alex) and Robert Moses (behind me). Photographer from governor's staff.

Alexander's swearing-in ceremony as Commssioner of Parks and Recreation. Left to right: Winthrop W. Aldrich, Laurence Rockefeller, and Alexander Aldrich.

The following summer, Arvis Chalmers, the *Knickerbocker News* columnist who specialized in Albany political gossip, called my office to do an article on the luxurious bathroom prepared for Governor Rockefeller's cousin. We offered him the opportunity to inspect the facility, and to use it if he wished, but we took the towel out before he came over. I don't think he took a shower, but he did pen an unfriendly article.

I called a staff meeting to get down to business. My first act was to select a secretary to record the minutes for the meeting. I asked Bob Young, an old hand on the staff who knew everyone there, to do that job, and I found out later that he bitterly resented having to do that kind of "women's work!" In later meetings, I rotated the role around the staff, including myself, and hoped Bob got the point!

My next act was to ask the entire staff what they believed to be our biggest challenge. Like a shot, Larry Logan, our tough, sardonic Irish attorney, barked back, "the Lewiston Theater!" Everyone nodded.

From 1949 until he retired in 1972, Earl W. Brydges had been state senator from the Niagara Falls area. In 1966 he became majority leader. His management style was firmly gentle, and his budgetary philosophy was absolutely clear: anything downstate had to be matched by something for the Niagara Frontier. Thus a bridge in Westchester County had to be matched by a major highway from Niagara to Oswego; a grant to fix up the Brooklyn Bridge required balance by a huge sound system for Lewiston's theater.

Erected on a landfill created by the spoils that came from the Niagara pumped storage power plant several years earlier, placed on top of a chemical waste dump, the Lewiston Theater resembled a power plant on the outside, but on the inside was one of the most sophisticated and expensive performing arts facilities in the whole state. Except for the long term support of Earl Brydges, there was no earthly reason for the selection of that place for a huge performing arts center. There was no local orchestra, no audience, no particular tradition for the arts, and very few community leaders who had any interest in it. Even the regional park commission, which included several community leaders, was reluctant to get involved!

I immediately called on everything I had ever learned in my prior political and social experience. I created a small professional staff of experts to help me decide what to do. I appointed Mark Lawton, my deputy for historic preservation, to lead the project, and it proved a brilliant choice. He searched for an arts expert, and we decided on Omar Lerman, who had just departed from running the Rochester Ballet. I selected Linda Adams, a young, capable and tough graduate of Skidmore College, who had once been a summer babysitter for my children and who had also done some work for my congressional campaign. Her most recent job had been running an arts program for the Brooklyn borough president, Abe Stark. Astonishingly, she was born and raised in Lewiston.

I gave the team the job of researching the entire region, and they found that a large part of the Canadian population resided within a two-hour drive of Lewiston. If we could create a unique tourist destination, people would come!

The team came up with a completely new idea: a theme park for the arts. Nobody in either country had ever proposed such an idea. Finally, they developed the idea into a wonderfully persuasive three-page presentation for Nelson Rockefeller.

Page one was a dreary photograph of Lewiston Theater, with a huge price tag on it inscribed "$7.5 million" along with a "for sale" sign, and a chain link fence around it. The page was entitled alternative number one.

The second page was the theater alone, and nothing else. No audience, no sponsors, no customers.

The third page showed our team's concept: a busy boardwalk with painters, sculptors, musicians, jugglers and every kind of vendor, along with huge crowds of customers, and the theater in the background. We polished the presentation carefully, and then Mark, Omar, Linda and I took it to Nelson at his office in New York City.

His first reaction was one of horror at the price tag! He reached out and tore it off the page and made us promise never to show it to anyone. In a remarkable show of chutz-pah, Omar asked him to sign it for him! Nelson, with a great demonstration of reluctance, said "For you, I will!" and he did, his full name written out, and handed it over. He then went on to approve the third alternative and gave us the go-ahead.

There were times later when some of us wished he hadn't. But for the next five years Artpark became our proud-est achievement.

The New York State parks system was huge, and when I arrived it was more than fifty years old. It consisted of 120 parks ranging in size from thousands of acres, like Alleghany on the Southern Tier, to a half acre, such as Bannerman's Island in the Hudson River. Some parks like Jones Beach and Bear Mountain served thousands of people a day. Some were hardly ever visited, like Breakneck Ridge in the Hudson Highlands, notorious for the rattlesnakes that haunted it. A few were regional parks before the state system was founded in 1924, including Letchworth, south of Rochester, and Niagara Reservation at Niagara Falls. Some were new when I arrived, notably Roberto Clemente State Park on the banks of the Harlem River in The Bronx, which I helped to dedicate. Several others were still under construction, including a hugely expensive park atop a vast sewage disposal plant in Harlem, sticking out from West 125th Street. A few boasted elaborate hotels, such as the Gideon Putnam in Saratoga Springs, the Bear Mountain Inn in the Hudson Highlands, and the Glen Iris on the falls of the Genesee River.

I decided very early in my service to the parks to make it a point to visit every single one of them, not only as an official visitor but also as customer, to actually partake of the services the park rendered. Thus I actually skied cross-country at Thatcher Park, swam at Bear Mountain and Jones Beach, took in symphonies and ballets at Saratoga Spa, and enjoyed the show at Jones Beach. I stayed at every park hotel, including Bear Mountain Inn and the Glen Iris at Letchworth, a rustic camp at Alleghany, and I docked at every marina throughout the entire system aboard my own boat, *Strider*.

I always paid the full price of my visits, and often learned things that I never would have been told had I not gone as a customer. Being a new administrator in a long-established agency is very different from starting a whole new program. First I had to establish the fact that I wasn't Robert Moses and I intended to run things differently than he had. Then I had to learn enough so that my decisions were sound.

For example, there was a First World War army base named Camp Upton, quite far out in Suffolk County, near a hamlet named Yaphank in the Town of Brookhaven. One day when I was still visiting parks all over the state, President Nixon decided to deaccession Camp Upton to the State of New York, and offered to send his daughter Julie up to hand over the deed to Governor Rockefeller.

It was arranged to have me join the party as commisioner, along with Laurance Rockefeller, as chairman of the State Council of Parks, because it had been decided to turn the Upton site into a state park. I was told to join the Rockefeller brothers at the East River Heliport. On a brilliant, sunny morning, we crammed into the back seat of a tiny, bubble-nosed chopper, and roared out about seventy miles to Yaphank. Startlingly beautiful and very gracious, Julie gave Nelson the deed, posed for pictures, and then we said goodbye and roared back to Manhattan.

The entire way back, Nelson and Laurance revealed their latest ideas to me about state parks. In effect they said, "We have decided to turn the Erie Canal into a new state park! You handle the details." Arriving back at the East River Heliport, when our pilot stopped the engine, the port-side door popped open and I fell to the tarmac. It had been open the entire trip, and I could as easily have fallen out over Mineola at three thousand feet.

At our next staff meeting, I asked the entire staff for help in planning for a canal-length park. I had a general idea that the canal was pretty much the same its whole length—a narrow ditch, with occasional locks, and pathways on each side that had been used in the past by a mule named Sal to tow the barges. I envisioned a user-friendly statewide bicycle

My last hurrah as Parks Commissioner, February 1979, Dartmouth College photographer. Five nights and days through Chateaugy Wilderness of Vermont. Temperature minus 20 degrees Fahrenheit. Pack weight 40 lbs. Cross-country skis. Sponsor, Hurricane Island Outward Bound survival program. I was 40 years old.

Lesson #1: "If you start ot fall (and you will), twist so you land on the pack!"

path, with scattered water access, and lots of small picnic areas that local people could enjoy. I shared these thoughts with the staff, and they all nodded wisely as if the commissioner was a genius.

On my next trip to Syracuse, I planned to present the idea to the Chamber of Commerce there but fortunately, before

I did so, I shared the idea with our regional administrator in that area, Samuel Perry.

"Bad idea!" Sam said. "In Central New York, almost the whole route is along rivers: the Mohawk, the Oswego, various lakes. In the springtime the banks flood, and a bike trail would be unusable.

I put my plan in my pocket.

I expressed my dismay with the staff at the following meeting, and then did what I should have done first: asked them to form a small committee to come up with a smarter plan.

This they did, and handsomely. They had the idea of designing recreation areas at as many locks along the canal that had enough land to handle them, and use them as the first steps in a process of converting the entire canal to a recreation destination. They also suggested that maybe I should also confer with Ray Schuler, the rather testy, Syracuse-educated engineer who had jurisdiction of the entire canal as commissioner of public works.

When I broached the subject to Ray, I discovered that neither Laurance nor Nelson had given him the word yet. Naturally, he was appalled at the idea, and said he would oppose me in the legislature! I gently told him it was not my idea but Nelson's, and I suggested that he speak with him about it.

He did, and the upshot was that we agreed that we would give the chief lock superintendants along the canal the opportunity to allow their locks to open to the public, under the supervision of OPR recreation people. Many of these men were extremely suspicious of the public, and wanted no part of the idea.

We did a survey, and found that only five lock "supers" were really enthusiastic about it. These were men who were proud of their locks and wanted to show them off.

I had to recruit and train a staff for the purpose, and I decided to sign up the first class of female park managers in the history of the system. They were all experienced in recreation, and were young and enthusiastic. Some of the older "parkies" from the Moses era disapproved, but the idea was one whose time had come.

We opened five lock parks the following summer. One was at Lock Number 4 on the Champlain Division, near Stillwater in Saratoga County. Naturally, I visited it frequently with my children.

The only other one I remember was in Brewerton, at the western entrance to Oneida Lake. A huge crowd showed up on opening day, as well as an apparently friendly TV reporter. He called me over to the microphone, and his first question was, "How do you justify the cost of this park?" Clearly, his station was dominated by conservative, anti-Rockefeller interests.

Smiling, my reply was, "The only capital expense was to build a fence to keep people from falling into the lock. The only operating expense is to employ our new park manager. We have a thousand people here today, and we have to be concerned with their safety! I would remind your viewers that this facility was completed in 1825, and has been opened to the public for the first time, today. This park system does not waste state money!"

I resisted the temptation to push him into the lock.

Artpark was our most important challenge throughout the first years of my service as commissioner. After getting Nelson's approval, it took a couple of years of intensely hard work to build a boardwalk, hire an administrator, and create the program for Lewiston's Artpark. Mark Lawton and Mark Lyon of the Albany staff, and Omar Lerman and Linda Adams, our consultants, did a heroic job pulling it all together.

Dale McConathy was the new director. He was an established arts administrator, but he was a prima donna who apparently could not abide women. Linda, who actually lived in Lewiston, would occasionally deliver instructions from Albany to him. He couldn't take this, and finally complained to the press that he would no longer take orders from the commissioner's babysitter.

A Buffalo paper sent a reporter to check the story. I cheerfully said it was true, she had cared for my kids for two years while a student at Skidmore, and had gone on to work for my political campaign, and then again in my Fifty-fifth Street office when I was Nelson's executive assistant. Then I told him she had served Abe Stark, Brooklyn borough president, as his coordinator for the performing arts. I said that Linda had always earned my complete confidence, and that McConathy still had not.

That ended the meeting, and the story never hit the paper.

I guess the word got back to Dale, for he quieted down and worked hard enough to put on a good opening night in July 1964, and it was smashing.

The Buffalo Philharmonic played beautifully, and the two headline artists were Ethel Merman, the Broadway singer, and Edward Villella, the incredible principal dancer of the New York City Ballet.

I went backstage and down the corridor to the performers' dressing rooms. I knocked on the first one, and when she said "Come in!" I entered and met a stout, sad-looking housewife surveying herself with distaste in a mirror.

"Miss Merman?" I said, "have you ever met Eddie Villella?"

"EDDIE VILLELLA!" she shrieked. "NO! HE'S HERE?"

"Stay right here, I'll bring him to you!" I said. She started to make up her face as I went down the hall.

I knocked on Eddie's room, which was two doors away, and asked him if he would like to meet Ethel Merman.

"ETHEL MERMAN!" he bellowed "MY GOD!"

"Follow me!" I replied.

Moving slowly so she would have enough time to make a few repairs, I escorted the shaken dancer down the hall, knocked on the door, and made the introductions.

She looked like Ethel Merman again, but both stars were absolutely speechless in the presence of each other. They were both in awe!

The evening's finale was a colossal fireworks display, first on the New York side and then answered from the Canadian side of the Niagara River, but both displays paled in comparison to the performances of Ethel and Eddie. Stardom must inspire, for they were both at their best, and they were watching each other from the wings.

That same summer a group called the Colorado River Runners called me for permission to use their vessels as a commercial venture to navigate the rapids on the Niagara River below Niagara Falls between Niagara and Lewiston. They needed to launch at the small pier that the park owned just below the American Falls. I told them they could, but they had to test the idea thoroughly first, and I would like to be aboard the first boat.

They came over from Colorado, tried it out once in their own craft, and then invited me aboard with a few others. The vessel was an enormous Avon inflatable raft with a 270-horse outboard on the stern. It appeared able to survive absolutely anything a river could throw at it.

I was clad in a slicker with a hood, and slicker pants with suspenders. Knee boots under the pants. An enormous Mae West life jacket. The whole outfit was bright orange. I thought it might be overkill, but you can never be too safe!

We pushed off into surprisingly tranquil but fast-moving water, turned the corner a half mile downstream, and were confronted immediately with a colossal haystack of water, boiling ominously, and our skipper went directly at it at high speed. He took us over the rock that caused it, and right through the waterstack. Beyond was an appalling succession of other haystacks, and he took us through them all. I held my breath through each one, and we somehow survived. The Avon bucked like a fat bronco, and the lines that crisscrossed its top would slacken and snap tight, but if you held on tightly enough you could stay aboard. I have to admit I was pretty frightened!

We landed at downtown Lewiston, met by a worried park staff with a welcome pot of hot coffee. I hastened to sign a permit, enabling the river runners to operate. The program started the following week. All who came aboard had to sign a release stating that they understood the risks involved, and absolving everyone concerned from liability. The very next boat was the first commercial effort of the newly formed Niagara River Runners. When it hit the first haystack, it turned over, dumped everyone into the river, and broke the wrist of a female passenger who immediately hired a local negligence lawyer. Notwithstanding the release she had signed, she won a judgment for damages, and the River Runners went back to Colorado. The program had lasted for one glorious day. But I can boast that I have shot the Niagara Rapids.

25

The King Funeral

For me, the end of the American Civil Rights Movement occurred very abruptly on April 4, 1968, when an insane white supremacist shot Dr. Martin Luther King, Jr. from a balcony at a motel in Memphis, Tennessee. This event was followed by a wave of race riots around the country. The Black Power Movement began to dominate the black response to white discrimination, and without King's sober, spiritual leadership, the SCLC could no longer unite whites and blacks to seek peace between the two communities. I immediately sensed that the role I had discharged since the fall of 1963 for Governor Nelson Rockefeller was over, and I felt very sad about it.

There was one event still to come, of course, and I went along for a final ride. Nelson and I were asked to attend King's funeral, five days after his death, at the Abyssinian Baptist Church in Atlanta. We flew down from Albany on Nelson's private plane, accompanied only by George Fowler, who had been with me throughout the Selma March and for King's 1963 "I Have a Dream" speech.

Met by a limo at the Atlanta airport, our arrival at the church caused no particular stir. A couple of ushers came out, escorted Nelson into the church where they were saving an honored guest seat for him, and instructed George and me to head down to the basement, to watch on closed circuit TV. The church was completely packed, and we meekly headed down the stairs.

Nobody else was down there, so George and I set out to explore. At the far end, we found a set of steps going up to a narrow door, which we figured let out behind the pulpit. George led the way. The door opened outward, and he had to shove a number of reluctant bodies out of the way. He slid in, reached back and pulled me in behind him. I shut the door, and we were both shoved back against it by the crowd he had displaced. For a brief moment, I was quite frightened that I was to be crushed.

Then I took stock of the situation. Immediately in front of me, and jammed up against me, facing me, held there by the crowd behind them, were three beautiful black women in their twenties, with bouffant hairdos, surrounding me with waves of expensive perfume. I began to wonder whether they might be Baptist angels sent by the Lord to collect Dr. King but then I began to hear the sonorous tones of Rev. Martin Luther King, Sr. coming from the pulpit right above me, and I calmed down.

I had no idea who the women were. I slowly eased my head around so I could whisper in George's ear, "Who are these ladies?"

He took his time. He whispered back. "The Supremes!"

By 1968, even I knew about The Supremes. Products of the Brewster-Douglas Housing Project in Detroit, created by Motown Records in 1959, in ten years' time they had crowded the Beatles off the best-seller charts. Their names were Diana Ross, Mary Wilson, and Florence Ballard; they were at the very height of their fame; I didn't dare move a muscle until the sermon ended.

We had to wait to become disentangled from the Supremes until the crowd in the rest of the church dispersed. I never had a chance to say either hello or goodbye to them. I have often wondered if they enjoyed that experience as much as I had.

Somehow I doubt it!

The rest of the day was anticlimactic. We found Nelson in the front of the church and we decided to join the rest of the huge crowd in a final Civil Rights march to the center of Atlanta. We somehow found his limousine, zoomed out to the airport, and I had supper at home that night.

26

The Road to Meadowbrook

When I was a student at St. Paul's School, one of my favorite passages in the Bible was Chapter 9 of the Acts of the Apostles, which recounts the conversion of Saul of Tarsus on the road to Damascus. At no point in my life have I experienced a real spiritual call to serve the Lord, but after reading that biblical account I always rather hoped that, when it did happen, it would happen just like that.

Many years later, during a special tour of Syria sponsored by the American University in Cairo, I actually traveled in a bus up that road, turned up the "Street which is called Straight" and visited the shrine where Ananias baptized Saul, and the scales fell from his eyes (Acts 9:11-12). Then I visited the wall where he, by then called Paul, escaped Damascus by being lowered down a wall in a basket (Acts 9:25). All this was historic and moving and interesting to me, but I experienced no conversion.

By February 1998, I had abandoned my teenaged expectation of having a big religious conversion with all the bells and whistles, with a modern-day Ananias standing by to relay the results to all my friends.

What actually happened seems to have been a little more prosaic.

During 1997, Phyllis and I built a new house on a lovely hill in the rural Town of Saratoga. By the end of the year it

June 2008, my 80th birthday celebration at the Episcopal Spiritual Life Center in Greenwich, N.Y. Photo by Tom Stock Photos.

First row, left to right: Hunter Watts, Wyatt Watts, Charlie Aldrich, George Aldrich, Sally Aldrich, Owen Murphy, Bridget Murphy, Sarah Murphy, Mayor Watts, Emma Watts.

Second row: Lucy Curell, Jennifer Aldrich, Barbara Watts, Sam Aldrich, Phyllis Aldrich, Cynthia Murphy, Brian Murphy, Flynn Aldrich, Thomas Watts.

Third row: Nick on top of Will Aldrich, Sarah Aldrich, Laine Atcheson, Winthrop Aldrich, Page Atcheson, Elizabeth Atcheson.

Back row: Alex Aldrich, Henry Curell, Patrick O'Bannon, Amanda O'Bannon, Taylor Watts.

was ready, and a final burst of effort in January allowed us to move in. Boxes of possessions were piled everywhere, and we faced a long process of unpacking even though we were both working hard in our respective jobs.

One morning in February during a snowstorm, Phyllis asked me to give her a lift into Saratoga Springs. It was a

Thursday, trash day, and I lugged some trash pails down the hill in the back of the car. I wasn't feeling well, and I noticed as I placed a few envelopes into the mailbox that my vision was acting strangely. I was having trouble focusing my eyes in such a way that I could see only one image; in fact, I clearly saw two, one on top of the other, as if one eye were aimed a tad lower than the other. That had never happened to me before, but I wasn't too concerned, because I had no pain.

I got back into the car with no trouble, and proceeded up Burke Road and crossed Fish Creek on Stafford's Bridge Road. I was still seeing two images. I turned left into Meadowbrook Road, and there I followed the wrong image and missed the turn! Phyllis bellowed. I jammed on the brakes and stopped before any damage occurred, and she said "You are having a seizure! Get out of the car!"

I was mildly indignant and said, "I'm *not* having a seizure!" But realizing that something had to be wrong, I dutifully opened the door and climbed down. My left leg collapsed and I knew that Phyllis was right—I was experiencing a stroke. Phyllis helped me around to the passenger side, and she drove right to Dr. Schwartz's office, across from the Saratoga Hospital Emergency Room. I managed to walk into his office with the assistance of an elderly black lady who saw I needed help, and for the next three weeks I was in a wheelchair.

There followed an incredible week of inquiry and coordination by Phyllis of all the myriad choices that faced us in seeking my recovery. I first remember Dr. Schwartz advising her not to have me admitted to a hospital, because I would receive better care at home. She explored Ellis Hospital in Schenectady, and home care, and a variety of other alternatives, and finally settled on keeping me at home, with a nice lady from a Schuylerville church who came every day and fed me lunch. My daughter Amanda came from Cincinnati, my son Win came from Maine, both to help unpack some of the boxes. The other children were too far away to help, but they all called in.

I wasn't much use to anyone during those first days. I remember a lot of tests, occasional visits from friends, trips to the neurologist in Glens Falls, and a gradual pattern of rehab sessions at the Wesley Health Center in Saratoga Springs. Rehab was a lot of hard work. I remember Father Don Gardner at St. George's Church advising me with his characteristic twinkle, "Nobody ever falls in love with their physical therapist—they're all too mean!" The Wesley women were never mean to me, but they were so excited to have a patient who was as determined as I was to get well again that they worked me as hard as I could stand it. I had a "small muscle" girl for fingers, a "large muscle" girl for legs, arms and balance, and a "larynx lady" named Janet Vavaseur who coached me to speak again.

Early in the treatment process, "fingers" urged me to learn to play the banjo. I could barely move my left wrist, let alone my fingers. A week or so later, I bought a banjo and forced myself to learn the fingering. Six months later, I brought the banjo back to the Wesley and forced her to listen to me play. We both agreed that Pete Seeger didn't have to worry, but I felt very proud of myself.

"Larynx Lady" Vavaseur gave me a cup of hot tea every morning when I went to visit her. I would choke every time, and I gradually realized that it was a test to see how I was doing. At a certain point, she recommended that I start to sing in a choir regularly, something I hadn't done since St. Paul's School. I signed up as a bass in the St. George's choir. I was so bad I was embarrassed, and decided to seek a voice coach. Happily, a member of the Bethesda Church choir, an attractive British soprano named Gwen Pykett, lived a few miles away from us, and for two years I spent an hour each week at her house, learning how to sing, to read choral music, to handle timing, and everything else that goes with effective choral performance. Then she and her husband returned to England, and I was glad to discover another marvelous coach, Steve Marking, who lives in Hoosick Falls and who has his own singing group to which I now belong. Thus, in my retirement, I have found a new purpose: singing for my own and other people's enjoyment.

Oh yes, by the way, I immediately realized that I could no longer meet the demands of my professorship at Empire State College. Meg Benke, director of the Distance Learning Program, and all my other friends and colleagues there were enormously sympathetic and helpful to us in arranging this, and I officially retired and began drawing my pension in due course.

Sarah, our youngest daughter, was at the time a student at Trinity College in Dublin. Months before the stroke, we had made reservations to spend Easter week in Ireland with her, and there was some doubt whether I could even consider going. At first I could not manage stairs, but after a couple of weeks I was able to do so, and Dr. Schwartz said I could make the trip. It meant a lot of help in airports, and I carried a cane. On one occasion, taking an elevator to the plane's special pilot's entrance in Dublin, but standing, I heard Phyllis exhort me: "Now look feeble!" It was quite easy to do so. We were there for a long week, visited Ackyll Island, Lisdoonvarna, covering about one thousand miles, and ate a lot of lamb chops. Sarah had made reservations everywhere, did all the driving, and I sat in the back seat, talking vapidly about what I was seeing out of the window. Sometimes I laughed myself to sleep in our motel room. I think I must have been exercising my mind to recover my old speech paths, or something like it.

I rapidly improved my muscular situation as spring approached, except in one area: my eyesight. The stroke had weakened the muscles in my right eye so that it now aimed down, giving me double vision. Of course I couldn't drive a car, and Phyllis had to taxi me around wherever I went. One evening, when I was still pretty much confined to home, my regular eye doctor, Dr. Mattison, made a *housecall*, carrying a pair of scissors and a sheet of fresnel lens paper. I knew from my navigational studies at Harvard that fresnel lenses were used in lighthouses to focus their lights into directed beams of light. They look like wrinkles on a sheet of glass. He took my regular day glasses, rotated the lens paper around so the light coming into my right eye compensated for the muscle spasm, and with my "new" glasses I could see well enough to drive. Mattison gave me a letter saying I could drive with spectacles. This delivered Phyllis from a daily burden, and also worked wonders on my own psyche.

But the underlying weakness in the eye muscle still had to be addressed. The problem was beyond the skills of my friends at Wesley. Dr. Soule, my neurologist, found the only optometric neurologist in the entire Capital District, Dr. Robert Fox in Schenectady. I went to him once a week for several months. The challenge was, of course, to exercise the eye muscles regularly. I would visit his office and perform a series of challenging visual tests, sometimes computer driven, that a patient therapist would operate with me. Between visits I sat at home, threw socks into a basket, spun tennis balls around my head on a string, and performed other exercises that tested my patience as much as my eyes. For months,

A happy retiree, 2009.

Author in costume for Cole Porter concert, aged 80, summer, 2008.
Taken by Phyllis W. Aldrich.

every morning I woke up to find that my eyes still didn't
focus. I went back to the drills and the doctor.

One morning, in July, I woke up and I saw only *one
image*. For a few days, when I got tired, the double images
came back, but then they disappeared, forever I hope!

By the end of 1998 I was pronounced more or less cured.
I became a Stephen minister that fall at St. George's, right
after starting to sing there. I gave up the banjo by popular
demand. I still exercise every other day, and I am healthier
and stronger than I was before the stroke. Throughout the
entire course of my illness and recovery, I have been awed by
the strength and support of Phyllis. She was, and continues

to be, amazing. Her loving support has kept me alive and restored my health.

And, another thing has happened, and that is why I have entitled this chapter "The Road to Meadowbrook."

I have always relished participation in the Episcopal liturgy, which I first experienced at St. Paul's, especially its music. Although admiring and respectful of my college roommate Rowland Cox and his commitment to Christ, I never before experienced the same thing in my heart of hearts.

The innate sort of skepticism I learned from my father and also from MIT and Harvard, seems to intrude on an uncritical acceptance of church doctrine. Moreover, my deeply ingrained sense of the ridiculous and tendency to see humor in what other people often pompously revere, makes me reluctant also. I have trouble believing the story of Shadrach, Meshach and Abednego in the fiery furnace, and of Jonah in the whale, and even some of Jesus' miracles. However, those months of illness and recovery have truly wrought a change in my spiritual view. Before, I was hoping that, when Christ needed me, He would call me, like He did Saul. I now feel, with some cautious, trembling uncertainty, that I need Him, more than He needs me. Might that turn out to be the conversion I have been hoping for?

Index